The Holy Spirit of God and The Great Adversary

Algernon J Pollock

Edited by John D Rice

Scripture Truth Publications

al Bible Truth Depôt,

d to Digital Printing

Second edition August 2017

ISBN: 978-0-901860-97-2 (paperback)

Copyright © 1944 The Central Bible Truth Depôt

Copyright © 2017 John D Rice and Scripture Truth Publications

Cover photograph ©iStockphoto.com/ratluk

Published by Scripture Truth Publications
31-33 Glover Street, Crewe, Cheshire, CW1 3LD

Scripture Truth is an imprint of Central Bible Hammond Trust, a charitable trust

Typesetting by John Rice
Printed and bound by Lightning Source

Foreword

Following our reprint of A J Pollock's "The Resurrection of the Lord Jesus Christ" in 2015, it was suggested that another of his publications, long out of print, deserved to be made available again.

Part 1, on the Holy Spirit, is an elaboration of a series of articles which first appeared in 1929 in the magazine *Scripture Truth*. As the misery of World War II continued unabated in 1944, the question arose in the minds of many Christians as to whether they were living in the Last Days. With his great ability to seize any opportunity to present relevant Bible-based teaching, A J Pollock penned Part 2, on the real Great Adversary, Satan.

On reading through, it was again apparent that, although the subject matter was very relevant to Christians today, its impact was blunted by words and phrases no longer in everyday use. This edition retains the general structure, argument and scripture references of the original, but presented in twenty-first century language. In preparing this edition for publication I have incorporated material from the original *Scripture Truth* articles where appropriate to clarify the text of the later publication, and as light a touch as

e and power of the
e you in the practical
enjoyment of the victory of the Lord Jesus over Satan at
the cross. As the author says in conclusion: "Not all
subjects in Scripture are pleasant, but all are profitable,
and for our learning." May you find it so.

John Rice

April 2017

Part 1: The Holy Spirit of God

The Person of the Holy Spirit

The Hebrew word in the Old Testament employed to designate the Holy Spirit of God, the third Person of the Holy Trinity, is *ruach*, signifying wind or spirit. The corresponding word in the New Testament is *pneuma*, likewise signifying wind or spirit.

When God chose to reveal Himself to mankind, He inspired men to commit His communications to writing. There is always a difficulty, in using the vehicle of human language, of giving full expression to Divine thoughts. Human language is designed to meet the needs and thoughts of men, and is bounded by time and sense. Divine thoughts, on the other hand, range far beyond the spheres of time and sense. To meet this difficulty, the Spirit of God has often stamped words, familiar to man in his ordinary speech, with a new and higher meaning. This was so with the words *ruach* (wind, spirit) and *pneuma* (wind, spirit). Quite plainly these words are often used in Scripture to designate a Person—the Holy Spirit of God. There is no difficulty in recognizing this in the Scriptures.

There is one particular passage of Scripture that shows how the ordinary word *pneuma* (wind, spirit) is used as a simile of the Spirit of God. We read our Lord's own words:

> "The wind [*pneuma*] blows where it wishes, and you hear the sound of it, but cannot tell where it comes from and where it goes. So is everyone who is born of the Spirit [*pneuma*]" (John 3:8).

I remember a very intelligent child asking his mother how could anyone know that he had a spirit, seeing it is invisible? The mother replied, "Mr. Pollock is coming to tea today. When he comes, we will ask him." In due time the question was raised. The spirit in man cannot be seen or weighed or located. It is said to be in our body. How can we know this? I said to the boy, "Have you ever seen the wind?" He answered, "No." I then asked, "Can you feel the wind?" He answered, "Yes." I replied, "That is like the spirit. Without our spirit we should be dead. The Bible says, 'The body without the spirit is dead.' You are not dead. That proves that you have a spirit." This answer quite satisfied the boy. It was his first introduction to the thought that existence can be apart from that which is material. The simile of the wind proved most useful. How apt the simile used by our Lord when He spoke to Nicodemus of the necessity of the new birth.

THE HOLY SPIRIT IS GOD

The Holy Spirit is GOD, equal with the Father and the Son in the unity of the Godhead, Three in One and One in Three, One in knowledge, purpose, power and will.

The Bible states facts, rather than setting out to prove them. For instance, the first four words in Scripture furnish us an example of this:

> "In the beginning GOD" (Genesis 1:1).

The name, God, is announced without any attempt at proof. Similarly, ranging through Scripture one finds facts, stupendous facts, stated in such fashion as to carry conviction to the mind of the reader, for each carries its own credentials.

The Scripture does not tell us in so many words: "the Holy Spirit is God". So let us briefly piece together scriptural testimony to this great truth. We shall find that the testimony is as convincing as if the Scripture *had* said in so many words, The Holy Spirit is GOD.

To begin with, the word GOD in Genesis 1:1 (as it is in thousands of cases throughout the Old Testament) is in the plural. The Hebrew language has three numbers—singular, dual, plural. The plural at the least must be three. Is there not seen clearly, in the fuller light that Scripture throws upon the opening verse of the Bible, the intimation of the Three Persons of the Holy Trinity—Father, Son and *Spirit*? Surely that much is clear.

Perhaps the most striking insistence on the unity of the Godhead (yet Three Persons in indissoluble unity) is found in the address to Israel:

> "Hear, O Israel: The LORD [*Jehovah*, singular] our God [*Elohim*, plural], the LORD [*Jehovah*, singular] is one!" (Deuteronomy 6:4).

One scarcely expects to find in the Old Testament the same clear unfolding of truth on this subject as is found in the fuller light of the New Testament. That waited for the time when our Lord should come into the world. However, there is one very clear passage in the Old Testament:

> "Come near to Me, hear this: I have not spoken in secret from the beginning; from the time that it

was, I [*Jehovah*, the I AM, an assertion of *Deity*] was there. And now the Lord [*Adonai*, plural] GOD [*Jehovah*, singular] and His Spirit [*Ruach*] have [*the Hebrew verb is singular*] sent Me" (Isaiah 48:16).

Here we have two Divine Persons sending forth a third Divine Person. This verse is truly wonderful. It deserves special study. The One sent claims to be from "the beginning", the I AM, Jehovah. He states that He is SENT by the Lord GOD and His Spirit. Here we have the sovereign action of two Persons of the Holy Trinity sending a third Person of the Holy Trinity—All acting in perfect harmony for a desired end, which is gradually unfolded for God's glory and the blessing of man.

Furthermore, it is interesting to observe how one Scripture harmonizes with another, though the writers may be separated by seven long centuries. The Apostle John supports this passage in his testimony. In that Gospel it is recorded how our Lord again and again referred to Himself as the SENT One. Here are four examples:

> "For He whom God has SENT speaks the words of God" (John 3:34).

*　　*　　*　　*　　*

> "The very works that I do—bear witness of Me, that the Father has SENT Me" (John 5:36).

*　　*　　*　　*　　*

> "I am from Him, and He SENT Me" (John 7:29).

*　　*　　*　　*　　*

> "That they all may be one, as You, Father, are in Me, and I in You; that they also may be one in Us,

that the world may believe that You sent Me" (John 17:21).

In the light of the above Scriptures, we can have no doubt as to the teaching of Isaiah 48:16, setting forth the truth of the Deity of the Holy Spirit.

Nor is this all. Other Scriptures fall into line. For instance, we read:

> "How much more shall the blood of Christ, who through the eternal Spirit offered Himself without spot to God, cleanse your conscience from dead works to serve the living God?" (Hebrews 9:14).

This adjective, eternal, constitutes the assertion of the Deity of the Holy Spirit, for God alone is eternal. It is remarkable that this adjective is used only in the case of the Spirit, and not in those of the Father and the Son, though the Deity of these is amply stated in the Scriptures.

Sovereignty, too, an attribute of Deity, is attributed to the Holy Spirit.

> "But one and the same Spirit works all these things, distributing to each one individually as He wills" (1 Corinthians 12:11).

This could only be affirmed of God, and here it is said of the Holy Spirit.

It has often been taught that the Holy Spirit is only an influence, thus denying His Personality. The Holy Spirit is a Person, and every person has an influence, but in the case of the Holy Spirit His Personality embraces omnipotence, omniscience and omnipresence. The

Personality of the Holy Spirit is clearly affirmed in Scripture.

> "The Holy Spirit said, 'Now separate for Me Barnabas and Saul for the work to which I have called them'" (Acts 13:2).

Here is a definite action by a definite Personality, and of such a character that it could only be attributed to God.

THE HOLY SPIRIT IS THE CREATOR

Creation is ascribed to the Holy Spirit:

> "By His *Spirit* He adorned the heavens" (Job 26:13).

Who but the mighty God could by a word spangle the heavens with untold millions of stars, many of them far larger than our sun? These stars are kept in their places by the Almighty Power that created them. Who but the mighty God could do this? This is in this Scripture attributed to the Holy Spirit.

It is true that creation in Scripture is generally attributed to the Son, the eternal Word:

> "All things were made through Him, and without Him nothing was made that was made" (John 1:3).

Once in Scripture is creation attributed to the Father:

> "There is only one God, the Father, of whom are all things, and we live for Him; and one Lord Jesus Christ, through whom are all things, and through whom we live" (1 Corinthians 8:6).

Creation is here equally attributed to the Father and our Lord Jesus Christ. The fact is, the Godhead is One in purpose and action. On such a subject as this, creation can be attributed equally to each Person of the Godhead.

How this proves that the Holy Spirit is God in full equality with the Father and the Son.

THE THREE PERSONS OF THE GODHEAD ARE BRACKETED TOGETHER IN SCRIPTURE IN FULL EQUALITY

The Father, Son and Holy Spirit are continually placed in Scripture on a footing of perfect equality. This is very plainly seen in the formula of baptism:

> "Go therefore and make disciples of all the nations, baptizing them in the name of the Father and of the Son and of *the Holy Spirit*" (Matthew 28:19).

Here, Father, Son and Holy Spirit in one name are alike invoked over each candidate for baptism.

When our Lord was baptized with the baptism of John we read:

> "When He had been baptized, Jesus came up immediately from the water; and behold, the heavens were opened to Him, and he [*John the Baptist*] saw *the Spirit of God* descending like a dove and alighting upon Him. And suddenly a voice came from heaven, saying, 'This is My beloved Son, in whom I am well pleased'" (Matthew 3:16-17).

Here we have a wonderful revelation of the Holy Trinity—Father, Son and Holy Spirit, One in counsel and plan for the blessing of man. This was surely designed to give the Man, Christ Jesus, His true place as the eternal Son of God in the eyes of John the Baptist, and of the repentant remnant who were present.

The well-known benediction brings the three Persons of the Holy Trinity together in a striking way:

"The grace of the Lord Jesus Christ, and the love of God, and the communion of *the Holy Spirit* be with you all. Amen" (2 Corinthians 13:14).

Again, the Apostle Peter brings the three together in similar fashion:

"Elect according to the foreknowledge of God the Father, in sanctification of *the Spirit*, for obedience and sprinkling of the blood of Jesus Christ" (1 Peter 1:2).

Here it would be well to give a word of warning. We might be inclined to look upon the Father as first in importance; the Son as second in importance; the Holy Spirit as third in importance. But this would be an utterly wrong thought. If the Father is God, He is supreme, and none higher. If the Son is God, He is supreme, and none higher. If the Holy Spirit is God, He is supreme, and none higher.

An illustration may help. Imagine a handsome chandelier with three branches, each branch equal in shape and size, each stretching out an equal distance from the central stem, each giving equal light from the same source. If the question were asked, Which branch is first in importance, which second, which third? you would rightly reply, No differentiation of this sort can be made.

But now suppose that, in order to be taken apart for cleaning and then correctly reassembled, the chandelier had to have its branches distinguished in some way. The branches might be numbered one, two and three, but that certainly would not designate any difference in importance. So it is with the subject before us. The baptismal formula gives us the Divine ordering of the name of the Father, Son and Holy Spirit. But to differentiate the one from the other on the lines of inequality would be very foolish and ignorant; and at worst, if the seriousness of this were understood, blasphemous.

The Holy Spirit in Old Testament times

It is remarkable that the first Person of the Holy Trinity to be mentioned in the Old Testament is the Holy Spirit of God. We read:

> "The Spirit of God was hovering over the face of the waters" (Genesis 1:2).

So *cosmos* was brought out of *chaos*. The ruined earth was brought into a suitable condition for the residence of man. Who was sufficient for this mighty work? Only a Divine Person.

As time went on we find men of God raised up. We find faith actuating Abel, Enoch, Noah, Abraham, Moses, David and many others. How was it that they were moved to live a life of faith? We read:

> "The just shall live by his faith" (Habakkuk 2:4).

It could only have been by the action of the Spirit of God. Man was under probation in the Old Testament, the children of Israel were under the law, affording the whole world a lesson, so that

"Every mouth may be stopped, and all the world may become guilty before God" (Romans 3:19).

But we also read,

"And the LORD said, 'My Spirit shall not strive with man for ever, for he is indeed flesh'" (Genesis 6:3).

How good it is that the Spirit of God strives with men, and how unutterably sad that they can resist until the awful moment comes when the striving ceases.

The time had not come for the full revelation of the truth of the Gospel. That waited for the coming into this world of the Son of God. But though the time had not come for this full revelation, we find God by His Spirit moving. On the ground of faith Abraham had righteousness imputed to him, and David knew the blessedness of sins forgiven. Who but one taught of the Spirit, could say,

"My heart shall rejoice in Your salvation" (Psalm 13:5),

*　　*　　*　　*　　*

"My heart is steadfast, O God, my heart is steadfast; I will sing and give praise" (Psalm 57:7)?

THE HOLY SPIRIT USED A WICKED MAN

"And Balaam [*the soothsayer, the spiritist medium, the covetous man*] raised his eyes, and saw Israel encamped according to their tribes; and the Spirit of God came upon him" (Numbers 24:2).

Was there ever a stronger proof of inspiration when a covetous man, who could have filled his house with silver and gold had he prophesied to please Balak, the King of Moab, was unable to do so? He was obliged to bless Balak's enemies when, left to himself, he would have cursed them. Not only was Balaam so energised but the

Lord opened the dumb mouth of his ass to rebuke the madness of the prophet.

THE HOLY SPIRIT EMPOWERED MEN FOR SPECIAL SERVICE

The Spirit of God is often mentioned in the Old Testament. The Holy Spirit came upon Gideon, Jephthah, Samson, Saul, David, and many others.

Pharaoh recognised that the Spirit of God was in Joseph when he said to his servants,

> "Can we find such a one as this, a man in whom is the Spirit of God?" (Genesis 41:38).

Then again, God called Bezaleel in connection with the construction of the Tabernacle and said,

> "I have filled him with the Spirit of God, in wisdom, in understanding, in knowledge, and in all manner of workmanship" (Exodus 31:3).

We read of Othniel, the son of Kenaz:

> "And the Spirit of the LORD came upon him, and he judged Israel" (Judges 3:10).

We read that

> "The Spirit of the LORD came upon Gideon; then he blew the trumpet, and the Abiezrites gathered behind him" (Judges 6:34).

We read four times that the Spirit of the LORD came upon Samson in connection with his mighty feats against Israel's enemies (Judges 13:25; 14:6, 19; 15:14).

There were three classes anointed with oil in Old Testament times—prophets, priests and kings. Oil is typical of the Holy Spirit, and, indeed, the Holy Spirit is called "the Anointing" in 1 John 2:27, and "an Anointing" ["an Unction", KJV (*same word as Anointing*)] in 1 John

2:20. When the prophet was anointed, it conferred upon him an endowment enabling him to fulfil the prophetic office. When the priest was anointed, it was an endowment to enable him to fulfil the priestly office. When the king was anointed, it was an endowment to enable him to fulfil the kingly office.

The case of Saul and David clearly illustrates this, showing the great difference between the sovereign action of the Holy Spirit in Old and New Testament times. King Saul, by his misconduct as king, had forfeited the right to reign. So God instructed Samuel to anoint David, a shepherd lad, the youngest of the sons of Jesse, in his place. We read:

> "Samuel took the horn of oil and anointed him in the midst of his brothers; and the Spirit of the LORD came upon David from that day forward. ... But the Spirit of the LORD departed from Saul, and a distressing spirit from the LORD troubled him" (1 Samuel 16:13-14).

This passage is very illuminating. It shows that the Spirit of God came upon men in Old Testament times for definite purposes, and for an indefinite time. Sometimes it was to strengthen them to slay their enemies, as in the case of Samson; sometimes to prophesy; sometimes to minister in the holy things of God; sometimes to rule over God's people, as in the case of David.

Here the Spirit is taken from Saul and transferred to David. After this, Saul is as a man bereft of God's presence and help. He seeks satanic help by consulting the witch of Endor, finally in the battle on Mount Gilboa dying ingloriously by falling upon his own sword. So ended a life that once had some promise in it. This shows that the Spirit could be given and withdrawn according to God's pleasure. In the New Testament the Spirit once bestowed is never withdrawn, as we shall see plainly when we take up that side of the subject.

David seems to have known that the Spirit of God could be withdrawn. After Nathan, the prophet, had rebuked David for his sin with Bathsheba, he wrote that great penitential psalm, when he cried out in the bitterness of his soul,

> "Do not cast me away from Your presence, and do not take Your Holy Spirit from me" (Psalm 51:11).

We must not imagine that the Old Testament characters mentioned in Hebrews 11 as men of faith were the only ones that were blessed. There must have been many more. Joseph's bough ran over the wall. Gentiles were blessed, as witness the names of Jethro, father-in-law to Moses; Job, the greatest man in the east; Naaman, the Syrian general; the widow of Sarepta, to whom Elijah was sent; and doubtless many others. God's Holy Spirit is sovereign and free.

The Holy Spirit in New Testament times

THE HOLY SPIRIT IN RELATION TO OUR LORD

We come now to the New Testament, to the great event of the birth of the Lord Jesus Christ into this world. First, our Lord as to manhood was begotten of the Holy Spirit of God. His parentage according to the flesh was unique. Born of a virgin, begotten of the Holy Spirit, He—who was, is and ever will be the eternal Son, the Son in the unity of the Godhead—became a true Man, yet never ceasing to be

"Mighty God, Everlasting Father" (Isaiah 9:6).

Such is the inscrutability of His Person, that He Himself declared,

"No one knows the Son except the Father" (Matthew 11:27).

His Manhood was holy and sinless.

"For He whom God has sent speaks the words of God, for God does not give the Spirit by measure" (John 3:34).

At our Lord's baptism at the hands of John the Baptist, we get the Holy Spirit's testimony as to His Divine mission in this world. Baptized (personally He did not need baptism), as identifying Himself in grace with those who had repented at the preaching of John the Baptist, He emerged from the water, when the Spirit of God like a dove abode upon Him.

> "John bore witness, saying, 'I saw the Spirit descending from heaven like a dove, and He remained upon Him. I did not know Him, but He who sent me to baptize with water said to me, "Upon whom you see the Spirit descending, and remaining on Him, this is He who baptizes with the Holy Spirit"'" (John 1:32-33).

We find how prominent the Spirit of God was in connection with our Lord's Manhood in this world. Begotten by the Holy Spirit of God, the Spirit given without measure, He was acknowledged at His baptism by the Holy Spirit.

This is all beautifully prefigured in the Levitical offerings. In connection with the grain, or meal, offering, which prefigures the beautiful life of our Lord, so pleasing to the Father's heart, we read:

> "And if you bring as an offering a grain offering baked in the oven, it shall be unleavened cakes of fine flour mixed with oil, or unleavened wafers anointed with oil" (Leviticus 2:4).

Oil in Scripture is emblematical of the Spirit of God. This is confirmed by John's first epistle speaking twice of the Holy Spirit as the Anointing. In the type here, unleavened bread typifies the pure and sinless humanity of our Lord. The cakes mixed with oil set forth how the Holy Spirit permeated our Lord's humanity through and through. The wafers anointed with oil set forth how our Lord was recognized publicly at His baptism at the beginning of His public service, publicly anointed for service.

This acknowledgment of our Lord in connection with His public service was maintained all through His service on earth. We recall how our Lord read from the Scriptures in the synagogue of Nazareth,

> "*The Spirit of the LORD* is upon Me, because He has anointed Me to preach the gospel to the poor. He has sent Me to heal the broken-hearted, to preach deliverance to the captives and recovery of sight to the blind, to set at liberty those who are oppressed, to preach the acceptable year of the LORD" (Luke 4:18-19).

The Spirit of God was the Power whereby as a dependent Man our Lord performed the wonderful acts of healing and mercy, by which He went about destroying the works of the Devil. No wonder that

> "All bore witness to Him, and marvelled at the gracious words which proceeded out of His mouth" (Luke 4:22).

When we come to our Lord's sacrificial death on the cross of Calvary, we may ask what is said of the Holy Spirit in that connection? Our Lord's atoning death was vitally necessary for our salvation, glorifying God, the very top-stone of Divine love, the righteous foundation of the universe of bliss we all look forward to. We read:

> "Christ ... through *the eternal Spirit* offered Himself without spot to God" (Hebrews 9:14).

This was a supreme act, and it was in the power of the Spirit that it was carried out to its glorious conclusion.

And what about the Lord's resurrection? Is anything affirmed of the Holy Spirit in that connection? We read:

> "If *the Spirit* of Him who raised Jesus from the dead dwells in you, He who raised Christ from the dead will also give life to your mortal bodies through *His Spirit* who dwells in you" (Romans 8:11).

This is a very striking and important Scripture. It brings out how the Persons of the Godhead act in perfect harmony. We read that our Lord was raised by the glory of the Father (Romans 6:4); that our Lord had power to lay down His life, and power to take it again (John 10:18); and now we have read a verse that states clearly that the Spirit of God acted in His resurrection. And not only so, the Spirit that raised Him from the dead is the Same that indwells the believer, as the pledge that as Christ was raised, so our mortal bodies shall be quickened at His coming again.

THE SPIRIT OF GOD WAS SENT INTO THIS WORLD TO INAUGURATE A NEW DISPENSATION

Our Lord in His closing days on earth spoke much of the Holy Spirit to His disciples. When He was about to ascend to glory, in all the efficacy of the work of redemption performed for our salvation, He told His disciples that the Father would send the Holy Spirit, the Helper, in His name, and He would teach them all things; that He Himself would send the Holy Spirit in the name of the Father, who would testify of Himself (Christ); that the Holy Spirit would come of His own initiative, and would guide believers into all truth, and would show them things to come (John 14:26; 15:26; 16:13).

28

THE HOLY SPIRIT AND THE DAY OF PENTECOST

A new day—the dispensation of the Church period—was inaugurated by the sending forth of God's Holy Spirit on that ever-memorable day. Pentecost was the day of the Church's birth, and with it went full provision. That day could not come until our Lord had glorified God at the cross by His expiatory sacrifice, not until He was risen from the dead and ascended to glory (Hebrews 1:3). Our Lord in His last days on this earth plainly indicated this when He said to His disciples:

> "Nevertheless I tell you the truth. It is to your advantage that I go away; for if I do not go away, the Helper will not come to you; but if I depart, I will send Him to you" (John 16:7).

Another Scripture makes it plain that our Lord must be glorified before the Spirit of God could be sent. We read:

> "This He spoke concerning the Spirit, whom those believing in Him would receive; for the Holy Spirit was not yet given, because Jesus was not yet glorified" (John 7:39).

We shall see the reason for this as we proceed.

All this is beautifully foreshadowed in the order of the feasts of the Lord as given in Leviticus 23. Among them we get the feast of

> "A sheaf of the first-fruits of your harvest" (verse 10).

This was to occur on "the day after the Sabbath". This must have been strange hearing in the ears of the pious Jew, who was taught so much about the Sabbath. Was not the Sabbath the day that was sanctified and set apart by God Himself in a very special way? But here it was emphasized "the day after the Sabbath". What could it mean? It will be plainly seen that it sets forth prophetically the resurrection of our Lord. He rose from the dead on the first day of the week, "the day after the Sabbath". He was *the first-fruits* of the whole harvest of grace that our God shall reap in the day of glory. We have the very word, *first-fruits*, applied to our Lord in that great resurrection chapter, 1 Corinthians 15:

> "But now Christ has risen from the dead, and has become *the first-fruits* of those who have fallen asleep" (1 Corinthians 15:20).

*   *   *   *   *

> "Each one in his own order: Christ *the first-fruits*, afterwards those who are Christ's at His coming" (1 Corinthians 15:23).

How blessed it is to see the fulfilment of the type of the waving of the sheaf of the first-fruits of the harvest in the resurrection of our Lord: the proof that not only does God accept our Lord as the One who satisfied Him as to the question of sin at the cross, but, by that act, Himself guarantees that the whole harvest of precious souls, every believer on the Lord Jesus Christ, shall be quickened in the day of His coming. If they fail to be accepted, it must be because He failed to be accepted. But we know He was accepted, and we, believers, are accepted in the Beloved. There can be no breakdown in this. How wonderful!

Fifty days after the feast of the first-fruits of the harvest came the feast of

> "A new grain offering to the LORD" (Leviticus 23:16).

This also is carefully noted as taking place "fifty days to the day after the seventh Sabbath". So we ask, what great event took place fifty days after our Lord rose from the dead, and is intimately connected with that resurrection. We know that our Lord was forty days on this earth after He rose from the dead, thus proving the wonderful fact of His resurrection to disciples, slow of heart to believe it. Before He ascended on high, He instructed His disciples to tarry at Jerusalem,

> "Until you are endued with power from on high" (Luke 24:49).

At last the fiftieth day arrived, a first day of the week. The record stands thus:

> "Now when the day of Pentecost had fully come, they were all with one accord in one place" (Acts 2:1).

Evidently there was a compelling force of the Holy Spirit gathering the disciples into one place for this wondrous event. The very word, *Pentecost*, comes from the Greek word, *Pentecoste*, meaning fiftieth. This clearly establishes the fact that the new grain offering was typical of the day of Pentecost when the Holy Spirit descended to form the Church of God on earth, and inaugurate this new dispensation.

This is further typified in the new grain offering. We are told it consisted of

> "Two wave loaves of two-tenths of an ephah. They shall be of fine flour; they shall be baked with leaven. They are the first-fruits to the LORD" (Leviticus 23:17).

The two loaves typified that Jew and Gentile would be one in Christ, and be an acceptable offering to Him. Nothing like this was ever known before. Baked with leaven is the recognition that believers were once sinful men and women, but the action of the fire would stop the working of the leaven, and the sin-offering accompanying the new grain offering sets forth how the atoning death of our Lord has met the sin question to God's glory and our eternal blessing.

Our Lord, before He left this earth, instructed His disciples,

> "Behold, I send the Promise of My Father upon you; but tarry in the city of Jerusalem until you are endued with power from on high" (Luke 24:49).

So the disciples gathered in an upper room, where they

> "All continued with one accord in prayer and supplication, with the women and Mary the mother of Jesus, and with His brothers" (Acts 1:14).

How expectant they must have been. What a wonderful moment in the history of the world! At length the fiftieth day after the resurrection arrived. Pentecost was a reality. From the glory, the promise of the Father was fulfilled. The risen and ascended Saviour sent in the Father's name the Holy Spirit of God, inaugurating this new and wonderful dispensation, the period of the Church's temporary residence on this earth. It was the day of the Church's birth.

It seems a mark of a fresh dispensation that it should be ushered in with impressive and outward signs. For instance, the exodus from Egypt was marked by ten plagues, ending with the death of the firstborn. The giving of the law from Sinai's smoking mount, so that even Moses feared and quaked exceedingly, was accompanied by terrifying sights and sounds. Our Lord's birth, His baptism, His death, and His resurrection were all accompanied with striking signs. We shall see that the day of Pentecost was no exception to this. It is striking that when the law was given, in the matter of the golden calf "about three thousand men" (Exodus 32:28) died; whereas on the Day of Pentecost "about three thousand souls" (Acts 2:41) were added to the Church.

The hundred and twenty disciples, more or less, were praying in expectation of this great event. It was "the day after the Sabbath", the first day of the week, the fiftieth day after our Lord rose from the dead, when

> "Suddenly there came a sound from Heaven, as of a rushing mighty wind, and it filled the whole house where they were sitting" (Acts 2:2).

We see again how the wind in a symbolic sense comes in as connected with the Holy Spirit, as we shall see when we take up the question of the new birth and our Lord's dealing with Nicodemus. Then an astonishing thing happened:

> "There appeared to them forked tongues, as of fire, and one sat upon each of them" (Acts 2:3).

We recall when our Lord was baptized by John the Baptist, as identifying Himself with the repentant remnant, that the Holy Spirit in the likeness of a dove rested upon Him. The dove symbol, the bird of peace, shows that there was nothing contrary to the Holy Spirit in our Lord, and therefore the Spirit could come upon Him in that way. In the Levitical type, the oil (symbol of the Holy Spirit) was put upon the blood. Sinful man could only receive the Holy Spirit on the ground of the atoning sacrifice of our Lord, the efficacy of the precious blood that cleanses from all sin. But in the case of our blessed Lord, the Spirit could come upon the flesh of our Lord, because His humanity was perfectly sinless and pleasing to the heart of the Father. But in the case of the believers on the day of Pentecost we read of "forked [cloven, KJV] tongues, as of fire" descending upon them.

The mark of a clean animal under the Levitical law was the combination of the characteristics of chewing of the cud and cloven hooves:

> "You may eat every animal with cloven hooves, having the hoof split into two parts, and that chews the cud, among the animals" (Deuteronomy 14:6).

The chewing of the cud is symbolic of meditation, a real *heart* appropriation of divine things, without which there would be no incentive or desire to part from worldly thoughts and ways, symbolized by the cloven hooves.

God would thus teach His ancient people that they should be holy people, clean people, if they would have to do with Him. Likewise, the Holy Spirit would teach this same lesson to Christians. Separation in heart and ways from the world that rejected our Lord is inculcated throughout the New Testament. The fire speaks of the Holy Spirit not allowing what is offensive to God in the believer's walk and ways. Fire is a destructive agent. Its work is purifying by destroying that which is offensive. We read,

> "Each one's work will become manifest; for the Day will declare it, because it will be revealed by fire; and the fire will test each one's work, of what sort it is" (1 Corinthians 3:13).

The result of these tongues of fire descending on the disciples was that

> "They were all filled with the Holy Spirit and began to speak with other tongues, as the Spirit gave them utterance" (Acts 2:4).

It seems as if one of the grand objects of the Holy Spirit's indwelling is the systematic spreading of vital information. Overriding the limitations of the Tower of Babel, when man's language was confounded so that they could not understand each other's speech, here we have the spectacle of the apostles speaking many languages, so that all heard in their own tongue the wonderful gospel of the grace of God. Strangers from many parts—Parthians, Medes, Elamites, dwellers in Mesopotamia, Judæa, Cappadocia, Pontus, Asia, Phrygia, Pamphylia, Egypt, Libya, Cyrene, strangers from Rome, Jews, proselytes, Cretans and Arabians—made up a most cosmopolitan audience. Yet from the lips of Galileans, fishermen mostly, "uneducated and untrained men", all heard the story of redeeming love in their own tongue. They were amazed and well they might be. It is no wonder that about three thousand souls were converted to God on that memorable day of Pentecost. Thus was inaugurated the descent of the Holy Spirit of God, bringing with it such wonderful blessing in this world.

Hitherto the testimony had been confined to Israel. Even our Lord said,

> "I was not sent except to the lost sheep of the house of Israel" (Matthew 15:24).

But now the news had to go world-wide, and the apostles received these instructions,

> "Go therefore and make disciples of *all the nations*, baptizing them in the name of the Father and of the Son and of the Holy Spirit, teaching them to observe all things that I have commanded you" (Matthew 28:19-20).

THE HOLY SPIRIT IN RELATION TO THE WORLD

It is said of the Spirit of God,

> "Whom the world cannot receive, because it neither sees Him nor knows Him; but you know Him, for He dwells with you and will be in you" (John 14:17).

There is a great division between the believer and the world. As our Lord said twice of His disciples in His prayer to His Father,

> "They are not of the world, just as I am not of the world" (John 17:16).

We read our Lord's own words in relation to the Holy Spirit, that

> "When He has come, He will convict *the world* of sin, and of righteousness, and of judgment" (John 16:8).

How does this happen? He provides proof

> "of *sin*, because they do not believe in Me [*the Lord Jesus*]" (John 16:9).

Why is the Holy Spirit in this world in the special way in which He is? Because Christ is rejected. Why is the Holy Spirit given to some and not to others? Because some believe and some do not. This marks the difference between the believer and the world, and it demonstrates the guilt of the world.

The Holy Spirit provides proof

> "of *righteousness*, because I go to My Father and you see Me no more" (John 16:10).

Christ is the righteous One, and the world proved its unrighteousness by rejecting Him. Righteousness is with the Father, and the descent of the Holy Spirit, consequent on the ascension of our Lord, is the proof of the world's unrighteousness. They rejected Him whom heaven acclaimed. Everything is out of joint in this world to those who love the Lord, just as the affairs of a kingdom would be out of joint to every loyal subject if the lawful king were driven out and a republic set up in his place.

The Holy Spirit provides proof

> "of *judgment*, because the ruler of this world [*Satan*] is judged" (John 16:11).

If Satan really had the upper hand there would be no Holy Spirit here; neither the Holy Spirit nor those whom He indwells would be tolerated in this world. How cheering is the word,

> "You are of God, little children, … because He [*the Holy Spirit*] who is in you is greater than he [*Satan*] who is in the world" (1 John 4:4).

That may be said of the feeblest or youngest believer in whom the Holy Spirit dwells. Wonderful words!

The Acts of the Apostles narrates the wonderful energy of the Spirit of God. The door of blessing was opened to the Gentiles when Peter preached to Cornelius and his friends. Saul of Tarsus was miraculously converted, and commissioned to be the Apostle *of* THE GENTILES. His activity was incessant. Wherever he went he left a track of blessing behind. Jews and Gentiles were converted on every hand, assemblies were formed, Christianity was established in the world. So great was the power of the Spirit of God in the preaching of the Word of God, that it was said of the evangelists Paul and Silas,

> "These who have turned the world upside down have come here too" (Acts 17:6).

Ever since that day the gospel has been winning its peaceful triumphs. Century after century rolls on. So also the work of the Lord. St. Augustine, Bishop Paulinus, Huss, Wyckliffe, Luther, Calvin, Knox, Wesley, Whitefield, Spurgeon, Moody and thousands besides bear testimony to the driving force of the Spirit of God in the proclamation of the Divine good news. Then there is the great missionary movement of more modern times. Carey, Duff, Moffatt, Livingstone, Hudson Taylor, Bishop Hannington, C. T. Studd and thousands more testify to the driving force that will cross oceans and brave martyrdom in the quest of seeking the perishing and lost for the kingdom of God.

The Holy Spirit and Salvation

THE HOLY SPIRIT AND THE NEW BIRTH

We come now to the consideration of the Holy Spirit's action in regard to the individual. Who takes the first step in blessing? Who seeks first, God or the sinner? Assuredly it is God that takes the first step. It was God who designed the gospel of His grace from first to last. It was God who sent His only begotten Son into the world to be the Saviour.

That God takes the first step is well illustrated in the case of Nicodemus. He was a ruler of the synagogue, a man of high religious position, an expounder of the law of Moses. He came to our Lord by night to ask questions, when he was met with the startling statement of our Lord:

> "Most assuredly, I say to you, unless one is born again, he cannot see the kingdom of God" (John 3:3).

No natural sight could see this spiritual kingdom. A new nature, with power to recognize it, was necessary for that.

Nicodemus thought only of the material side, and was puzzled, and no wonder. Our Lord spoke of a realm of things clean outside merely human knowledge and experience. Nicodemus asked in astonishment,

> "How can a man be born when he is old? Can he enter a second time into his mother's womb and be born?" (John 3:4).

Throwing further light on the subject, our Lord answered,

> "Unless one is born of water and the Spirit, he cannot enter the kingdom of God" (John 3:5).

Our Lord thus told Nicodemus that the entrance into the kingdom of God was effected by the instrumentality of the water and of the Spirit.

Many teach that "water" here refers to the rite of baptism. But this is not so. There was no Christian baptism known at the time our Lord spoke, but that which was administered by John the Baptist, "a baptism of repentance for the remission of sins" (Luke 3:3), in view of the coming Messiah. Also, our Lord's disciples baptized on the same lines. Christian baptism was not yet known. That was dependent on the death and resurrection of our Lord, and believers are "buried with Him through baptism into death" (Romans 6:4). Nothing of this was known when our Lord spoke to Nicodemus.

To teach that this "water" refers to baptism may suit the ritualist, and a priesthood who would thereby attribute to themselves a power which, if true, would make baptism a necessary rite for entrance into the kingdom of God, thereby putting great power into their hands. If this were "water" baptism, then the dying thief could not go to Paradise for he was never baptized. Nor could Abraham, Moses, David, Isaiah, or any of the men of faith in the Old Testament times.

However, we are not left to wonder what this refers to. Scripture itself makes it plain. We read,

> "Christ also loved the church and gave Himself for her, that He might sanctify and cleanse her with *the washing of water* BY THE WORD" (Ephesians 5:25-26).

So we find the simile of "water" is used to designate the Word of God. The Apostle Peter confirms this, though his simile is that of "incorruptible seed".

> "Having been born again, not of corruptible seed but incorruptible, *through the word of God* which lives and abides for ever" (1 Peter 1:23).

*   *   *   *   *

> "Of His own will He brought us forth *by the word of truth*, that we might be a kind of first-fruits of His creatures" (James 1:18).

Thus Scripture itself settles for us what is meant by "water and the Spirit", even the Holy Spirit of God using the Word of God for the impartation of divine life. It comes about by no human hands but is the sovereign action of the Spirit of God.

Our Lord went still further in unfolding the truth of this new birth to Nicodemus.

> "The wind blows where it wishes, and you hear the sound of it, but cannot tell where it comes from and where it goes. So is everyone who is born of the Spirit" (John 3:8).

Here is emphasized the sovereignty of God in this matter. The new birth is like the blowing of the wind. Where it comes from, and whither it goes is beyond human control. So with the new birth. We are begotten of *God's* will. God takes the initiative. We are thankful that it is so.

It is true that God uses the Word of God in the matter of the new birth. We read,

> "Having been born again, not of corruptible seed but incorruptible, through the Word of God which lives and abides for ever, because 'All flesh is as grass, and all the glory of man as the flower of the grass. The grass withers, and its flower falls away, but the Word of the LORD endures for ever.' Now this is the word which by the gospel was preached to you" (1 Peter 1:23-25).

It is GOD who uses it in sovereignty, and it is the same Word that in the preaching of the Gospel brings the glad news of forgiveness, and salvation.

> "But as many as received Him, to them He gave the right to become children of God, to those who believe in His name: who were born, not of blood, nor of the will of the flesh, nor of the will of man, but of God" (John 1:12-13).

THE HOLY SPIRIT IS THE GREAT SANCTIFIER

The Apostle Peter, addressing believers, describes them as

> "Elect according to the foreknowledge of God the Father, *in sanctification of the Spirit*, for obedience and sprinkling of the blood of Jesus Christ" (1 Peter 1:2).

Please note carefully that in this passage sanctification is put in order before the reception of the gospel. This is borne out by the Apostle Paul in a striking passage,

> "We are bound to give thanks to God always for you, brethren beloved by the Lord, because God

from the beginning chose you for salvation through *sanctification* by the Spirit and belief in the truth" (2 Thessalonians 2:13).

Here the order is very clear. The Spirit of God sanctifies, sets the individual apart for Divine blessing. From the beginning God chooses men for salvation. This is His sovereign act. Sanctification comes first, then belief of the truth, and so salvation is reached.

This is again emphasized by the same writer,

> "And such were some of you. But you were washed, but *you were sanctified*, but you were justified in the name of the Lord Jesus and *by the Spirit of our God*" (1 Corinthians 6:11).

Note the order here, sanctification comes before justification. What then does sanctification mean? In these passages it is the act of the Holy Spirit, and means the setting of the individual apart in the mind of the Spirit and by His work for Himself. It is often designated *absolute* sanctification as opposed to *practical* sanctification, in which latter the Spirit leads the believer to holiness of life in his practical ways as a Christian. This with all Christians is progressive as we learn ourselves and God—as we learn to distrust ourselves, and discover the incorrigible nature of the flesh, and learn God in all His holiness, who says to every Christian,

> "But as He who called you is holy, you also be holy in all your conduct, because it is written, 'Be holy, for I am holy'" (1 Peter 1:15-16).

The Holy Spirit of God dwells in holy people. We are to glorify God in our own bodies.

> "Flee sexual immorality. Every sin that a man does is outside the body, but he who commits sexual

immorality sins against his own body. Or do you not know that your body is the temple of the Holy Spirit who is in you, whom you have from God, and you are not your own? For you were bought at a price; therefore glorify God in your body and in your spirit, which are God's" (1 Corinthians 6:18-20).

*   *   *   *   *

"Do you not know that you are the temple of God and that the Spirit of God dwells in you? If anyone defiles the temple of God, God will destroy him. For the temple of God is holy, which temple you are" (1 Corinthians 3:16-17).

This is most blessed, yet most solemn. For us, who are indwelt by the Spirit of God, it is our duty to always remember what a tremendous claim to holiness lies upon us.

THE HOLY SPIRIT: THE ANOINTING, SEAL AND EARNEST

It is hardly necessary to say that the Holy Spirit comes to a believer once and once only. He comes, as our Lord said when near the end of His life on this earth, "that He may ABIDE with you for ever" (John 14:16). This was in contrast to Old Testament times when the Spirit might come and go, as for instance when "the Spirit of the LORD departed from Saul" (1 Samuel 16:14). With this agrees Ephesians 4:30, where it is said to the believers, "you were sealed *for the day of redemption*", that is until the glad day when our Lord shall raise His sleeping saints and change His living saints, when redemption shall even touch our bodies as it has our souls, and the flesh and mortality and corruption shall be left behind for ever.

There is then only one coming of the Holy Spirit to indwell the believer, though the one coming is looked at as from three different points of view as Seal, Anointing and Earnest.

These three aspects of the one indwelling of the Holy Spirit in the individual believer are mentioned in 2 Corinthians 1:21-22.

> "Now He who establishes us with you in Christ and has *anointed* us is God, who also has *sealed* us and given us the Spirit in our hearts *as a deposit*" (2 Corinthians 1:21-22).

These are three aspects of the one indwelling, setting forth the Spirit of God in His action towards the individual believer, as seen in different connections.

These could not be affirmed of the Old Testament believer. They are contingent on the death, resurrection, and ascension of our Lord, and His sending forth the Holy Spirit, inaugurating this present Christian dispensation. We shall see what wonderful privileges are involved, and their corresponding responsibilities.

Let us take them step by step, and examine the significance of each.

THE HOLY SPIRIT IS THE ANOINTING

The word, *anointing*, is used as a simile. The best explanations we can get are found in the Scriptures. There were three classes anointed in the Old Testament—priests, prophets and kings. They were anointed by oil being poured on their heads. This outward and ritualistic act was in keeping with the Old Testament system of worship as given by God among the children of Israel. But let it be carefully noted that along with the ritualistic anointing, there was a *spiritual* accompaniment.

This was well illustrated in the case of the anointing of David to be king over Israel by the prophet Samuel. We read,

> "Then Samuel took the horn of oil and anointed him in the midst of his brothers; and the Spirit of the LORD came upon David from that day forward" (1 Samuel 16:13).

So anointing in such cases was accompanied by something real. It was not just a mere bit of formalism, but carried with it the giving of the Holy Spirit according to the need of the one anointed.

Oil is a well-known type of God's Holy Spirit. In the case of the anointing of a priest, the Holy Spirit of God would give the one anointed the intelligence and power to carry out the priestly office. The anointing of the prophet would carry with it the intelligence and power to carry out the prophetic office. The anointing of the king would give him the intelligence and power to carry out the kingly office.

So it is with the Christian. True, in Christianity there is no warrant for any outward ritualistic act in anointing with oil in this connection. When this is attempted, Spurgeon said it was a case of empty hands upon empty heads. But the Christian anointing is the spiritual communication of divine intelligence and power to carry out the Christian life by the reception of the Holy Spirit.

We now present Scriptures to prove this statement. We read,

> "Because you are sons, God has sent forth the Spirit of His Son into your hearts, crying out, 'Abba, Father!'" (Galatians 4:6).

This is a most beautiful passage. It puts the matter before us in a wonderful way. The Spirit of God within us is the Spirit of God's Son. As such the Spirit of God shares with God's Son all the unfolding of the blessings that God the Father showers on His children. To have such a Spirit within us must mean intelligence and power for the believer. Such a Spirit puts the believer at home with Divine things, and the more he knows of them, the more it produces holy reverence and joy.

Again,

> "You did not receive the spirit of bondage again to fear, but you received the Spirit of adoption by whom we cry out, 'Abba, Father.' The Spirit Himself bears witness with our spirit that we are children of God" (Romans 8:15-16).

This again emphasizes the thought of spiritual intelligence. What a wonderful revelation that we can call God, Father; that we are the children of God. We have the intelligence for this and the power to take up the relationship. So we read our Lord's own words,

> "The Helper [*one called alongside to help*], the Holy Spirit, whom the Father will send in My name, He will *teach you all things*" (John 14:26).

"Teach you all things" is intelligence surely of the highest order.

The Apostle John emphasizes the same thought. Writing to "little children", that is, the babes in the family of God—those who are just beginning the Christian life—he says,

> "You have an anointing from the Holy One, and you know all things" (1 John 2:20).

This seems startling at first. It cannot mean that the immature babe, or even the most mature saint, knows everything. But, in having the Spirit, we have One indwelling who knows everything, and in every difficulty or lack of knowledge thus have a capacity to receive Divine teaching.

Again we read,

> "The anointing which you have received from Him abides in you, and you do not need that anyone should teach you; but as the same anointing teaches you concerning all things, and is true, and is not a lie, and just as it has taught you, you will abide in Him" (1 John 2:27).

Some have foolishly taken this verse to mean that they must not receive any teaching or ministry from any servant of the Lord. As a rule, those who come to this understanding of the passage are highly conceited, and vainly think that no person can teach them. We have come across such cases, men puffed up with fleshly pride, posing to be so high and mighty that no one can help them or teach them. They are *self*-sufficient, and that is to their condemnation.

One thing is certain. Scripture never contradicts itself. We have the passage which tells us of our Lord, the Head in Heaven, giving gifts to men—apostles, prophets, evangelists, pastors, teachers,

> "for the equipping of the saints for the work of ministry, for the edifying of the body of Christ" (Ephesians 4:12).

What is meant by the Apostle John is, that no man, as a *mere* man with *natural* powers only, can teach the believer anything. The wisest *scholar* in this world's learning, if unconverted, cannot teach the simplest believer one divine truth. The Spirit of God, working in the believer's heart, is able to teach the believer all truth. And even when we hear and receive teaching and ministry from the Lord's servants, they do not speak as merely natural men but as sanctified vessels for the presentation of truth, which the Holy Spirit must enforce on the minds of the hearers to make the ministry or teaching effective. It is the Holy Spirit of God who teaches. He is the only Teacher, but He graciously uses human vessels as His agents.

> "Behold, I send the Promise of My Father upon you; but tarry in the city of Jerusalem until you are endued with *power* from on high" (Luke 24:49).

We need power for living, for walking, for fruit-bearing, for witnessing, indeed for all the activities of the Divine nature, so we read,

> "If we live in the Spirit, let us also walk in the Spirit" (Galatians 5:25).

*   *   *   *   *

> "The fruit of the Spirit is love, joy, peace, long-suffering, kindness, goodness, faithfulness, gentleness, self-control. Against such there is no law" (Galatians 5:22-23).

THE HOLY SPIRIT AS SEAL

A seal is that which authenticates or ratifies, that which makes fast or secure, that which gives full assurance to a transaction. A seal is an engraved stamp used to impress or seal a letter, either to claim it as the property of the one who seals it, or as authorizing the one to whom it is addressed as alone entitled to break it. The Great Seal of the United Kingdom, for instance, is that which authenticates, and makes binding the laws of the British constitution.

Scripture affords us instances of the use of seals.

> "Then a stone was brought and laid on the mouth of the den, and the king sealed it with his own signet ring and with the signets of his lords, that the purpose concerning Daniel might not be changed" (Daniel 6:17).

* * * * *

> "The chief priests and Pharisees gathered together to Pilate, saying, ... 'Therefore command that the tomb be made secure until the third day ...' So they went and made the tomb secure, sealing the stone and setting the guard" (Matthew 27:62-66).

Woe betide anyone who would dare to tamper with these seals, but when the One who seals is God, who is omnipotent, omniscient, and omnipresent, the sealing is eternally effective, and no power in heaven, earth, or hell can tamper with it.

It is clear that the sealing is that aspect of the Holy Spirit's indwelling in which God is pleased to claim the believer for Himself once and for ever with a claim that is everlasting. The believer is

> "Sealed for the day of redemption" (Ephesians 4:30),

that is, till the coming of the Lord to take His own in a moment, in the twinkling of an eye. If a saint has died in the meantime, he will be raised at the second coming of our Lord, and given a body like unto Christ's.

The question may be asked,

WHEN IS THE BELIEVER SEALED?

Ephesians 1:13 furnishes a clear answer.

> "In Him [*the Lord Jesus*] you also trusted, after you heard the word of truth, the gospel of your salvation; in whom also, having believed, you were *sealed* with the Holy Spirit of promise."

This is a remarkable passage, demanding careful examination. Here we find that after they believed they were sealed. The important point to grasp is what they believed. We are told, "The word of truth, the gospel of your salvation." What is meant by "the gospel of your salvation"? The answer is, the good news that enabled them to know:

- their own *sinfulness* ["There is none righteous, no, not one" (Romans 3:10); "All have sinned and fall short of the glory of God" (Romans 3:23)];

- the *righteousness* of the Lord Jesus Christ, Son of God and Son of Man ["Jesus Christ the righteous" (1 John 2:1); "He was manifested to take away our sins, and in Him there is no sin" (1 John 3:5)];

- the *judgment* of God that Jesus bore for their sins upon the cross ["Christ died for our sins according to the Scriptures, and that He was buried, and that He rose again the third day according to the Scriptures" (1 Corinthians 15:3-4)];

- the *purpose* of the Word of truth ["These are written that you may believe that Jesus is the Christ, the Son of God, and that believing you may have life in His name" (John 20:31)];

and, hearing that Word, to believe, so that:

"When you received the word of God which you
heard from us, you welcomed it not as the word of
men, but as it is in truth, the word of God, which
also effectively works in you who believe"
(1 Thessalonians 2:13).

When a man or woman believes on Christ and receives
the testimony of His Word, that person is sealed by God's
Holy Spirit. Sadly, how many there are who, through
hearing "a different gospel, which is not another; ...
[from] ... some who trouble you and want to pervert the
gospel of Christ" (Galatians 1:6-7), have *not* heard the
Word of truth and so have not believed the "gospel of
their salvation".

A question was asked in a Bible reading concerning the
Scripture,

"In Him you also trusted, AFTER you heard the
word of truth, the gospel of your salvation; in
whom also, HAVING believed, you were sealed with
the Holy Spirit of promise" (Ephesians 1:13).

The question was, How long AFTER the believing does the
sealing take place? The answer given was, It is not a
question of time, but of *order*. Receive the gospel of your
salvation, receive the Spirit, the one is the consequence
following on the other. The illustration was used of the
blow of a sword and the resulting cut. The order could not
be reversed. There must be the blow of the sword first and
then the resulting cut. The stroke and the cut are one act.
When once a man or woman receives the gospel of their
salvation, that moment God gives the Seal of the Holy
Spirit, claiming the believer for Himself for ever.

We might ask, For how long is the believer sealed?
Ephesians 4:30 gives the answer, "And do not grieve the

Holy Spirit of God, by whom you were sealed for the day of redemption." Grieving the Spirit is a serious matter, but we cannot grieve Him away. Believers are sealed "for the day of redemption", that is, till the Lord comes and redeems our very bodies, when "in a moment, in the twinkling of an eye" we are with Him and like Him for ever.

THE HOLY SPIRIT IS THE EARNEST

The word, translated *"earnest"* in the Authorized Version, only occurs three times in the Scriptures.

> "[God] also has sealed us and given us the Spirit in our hearts as a *deposit*" (2 Corinthians 1:22).

*　　*　　*　　*　　*

> "God … also has given us the Spirit as a *guarantee*" (2 Corinthians 5:5).

*　　*　　*　　*　　*

> "You were sealed with the Holy Spirit of promise, who is the *guarantee* of our inheritance" (Ephesians 1:13-14).

The Greek word signifies a deposit, a part of a payment, given in advance as a guarantee that the whole will be paid afterwards. For illustration, when a house is purchased, it is customary to pay down a certain percentage of the purchase price to show that the purchaser means to complete the deal. When the seller gets the deposit, he knows that he will see the lump sum later on. The deposit shows that you are in earnest about the transaction.

In a similar way we, Christians, are in this world of sin and suffering and discipline. We are strangers and pilgrims on our way to the heavenly home where all shall be sinless and stainless. We have not arrived yet, but the assurance that we shall be there is given by the Holy Spirit. In other words, by the Spirit's power we taste now the joys that shall be ours in all their fullness when we get to glory.

We remember hearing a good illustration of the seal and earnest of the Spirit. Suppose a farmer goes to market and takes one of his men with him. He buys a few sheep, and gives orders to his man to put his mark upon them, so that they can be identified if they get straying or mixed up with sheep belonging to other owners. That is like the *sealing*. The sheep are bought and the farmer instructs his man to drive them home. On arriving it would be dark, so he instructs that they should be placed in the empty barn for the night and each given a few handfuls of clover to eat, and the next morning put in the clover field. Suppose the sheep could understand and express their thoughts one to another, would they not say as they were enjoying the clover in the dark barn, "If the clover tastes so good here in the dark barn, how good it will be to be in the clover field in the bright sunshine tomorrow?" The clover in the barn was the *earnest* of the field.

So, if we Christians enjoy the heavenly food the Holy Spirit provides for us now in the dark barn of this world, what will it be when we are in our proper sphere in the Father's house on high, enjoying these things without limitations? The following incident well illustrates this.

A good many years ago a Christian conference was being held in the United States of America. A lonely isolated Christian, who had very few opportunities for Christian fellowship, travelled a good thousand miles to be present. When he saw more Christians gathered together than he had probably ever seen before, his spirit was moved, and he asked the assembled Christians to sing the hymn beginning with the words,

> *"What will it be to dwell above,*
> *And with the Lord of glory reign,*
> *Since the blest knowledge of His love,*
> *So brightens all this dreary plain?*
> *No heart can think, no tongue can tell,*
> *What joy 'twill be with Christ to dwell."*

Joseph Swain (1761-1796)

The working of the earnest of the Spirit was plainly seen in what was filling his mind with joyful anticipation.

The Holy Spirit in the Believer's Life

THE HOLY SPIRIT TEACHES, TESTIFIES AND GUIDES

THE HOLY SPIRIT TEACHES

We read,

> "But the Helper, the Holy Spirit, whom the Father will send in My name, He will TEACH you all things, and bring to your remembrance all things that I said to you" (John 14:26).

This was said to the apostles who journeyed with our Lord when upon earth, but the principle stretches out to all God's people. The Holy Spirit is the infallible Teacher. How important then is our study of God's Word, which contains this teaching for our learning. We may rest assured that what the Holy Spirit taught the apostles is for us, and all things brought to their remembrance are found in the Word of God.

THE HOLY SPIRIT TESTIFIES

We read,

> "But when the Helper comes, whom I shall send to you from the Father, the Spirit of truth who

proceeds from the Father, He will TESTIFY of Me" (John 15:26).

This certainly is the test of the Holy Spirit's activity. Many, mainly of a charismatic persuasion, misinterpret the teaching of the Spirit, leading to believers being occupied with themselves, and with *their* own attainments, with *their* power, with *their* ability, perhaps to speak with tongues and perform divine healing, as they often claim. Christ is lost sight of in this mis-representation of one of the greatest and most blessed truths of Christianity, namely the true office of the Holy Spirit is to testify of Christ. What blessed occupation of the Holy Spirit it is to testify of our risen Lord. All truth centres round Him. He is the revealer of God, the Father; He is the Mediator between God and man; He is the Finisher of the work of redemption; He is the Giver of the Holy Spirit; He is Apostle and High Priest of our confession; He is our great High Priest and Advocate in heaven; He is the great Head of the church His body; He is the One who walks in the midst of the seven golden candlesticks; He is the Bridegroom, soon coming to claim His bride; He is the Judge of all the earth. We know this, and much more, by the Spirit.

THE HOLY SPIRIT GUIDES

We read,

> "However, when He, the Spirit of truth, has come, He will GUIDE you into all truth; for He will not speak on His own authority, but whatever He hears He will speak; and He will tell you things to come" (John 16:13).

Here the Spirit is the Guide. We do well if we do not bring our pre-conceived notions to the Word of God and endeavour to force Scripture to conform to our pet ideas.

We do well if we reverently take what the Spirit gives and follow His guidance.

There is some question as to what the words the Spirit "will not speak" mean in this verse. Some think it means that the Spirit will speak about the Father and the Son. but not *about* Himself. Others think it means that the Holy Spirit will not speak *of His own initiation*. The latter view is undoubtedly the truth. Greek scholars tell us there is no doubt that this is the force of the original. This is confirmed by the fact that a good deal of teaching concerning the Holy Spirit is found throughout the New Testament, notably Romans 8 and the Epistle to the Ephesians. The Spirit, in the wisdom of the Godhead, does not take an inferior position, but becomes the Power for the formation of Christian character, and the inspirer of prayer and praise and worship and of service to the Lord.

Then we read, "He will tell you things to come." What was to come? Christianity as we know it! The full unfolding of Christ and all that He brings to light, the teaching as to the individual saints, and to the assembly of God upon the earth, the prophecies of the future, whether it be the rapture of the saints of God to heaven, the unfolding of judgments on this world, the millennial kingdom of our Lord and the eternal state of blessedness, and all else that was to be revealed.

THE HOLY SPIRIT MAY BE GRIEVED

We read,

> "Do not grieve the Holy Spirit of God, by whom you were sealed for the day of redemption" (Ephesians 4:30).

In what way can the Spirit be grieved? Every allowance of the flesh in the walk and ways of the believer grieves the Spirit. The verses that circle round this passage show that it is largely through our tongues that we grieve the Spirit. The tongue gives vent to feeling inside. So we are warned against corrupt communications coming from our mouths, of bitterness, wrath, anger, clamour, evil speaking, malice. Let these things be put far away from the believer. It is when we find the flesh in others, that we so quickly find the flesh rising in ourselves.

THE HOLY SPIRIT MAY BE QUENCHED

We read,

"Do not quench the Spirit" (1 Thessalonians 5:19).

To quench the Spirit is to refuse to follow the leading of the Spirit, or to refuse to accept what the Spirit might give through others. For instance, if the Apostle Paul had refused the direction of the Spirit of God to preach the gospel among the Gentiles, the Spirit would have been quenched, and the greater part of the Acts of the Apostles would never have been written. The quenching of the Spirit might be: if the Spirit of God directed a saint to minister to the temporal needs of a poor saint, or even of an unbeliever, and he does not do so. In such a case the Spirit would be quenched.

Grieving the Spirit is through fleshly activity on my part; quenching the Spirit is through refusing the activity of the Spirit of God. Or it might be by a believer refusing to accept ministry, because the one ministering is not approved of.

Surely the Spirit of God was both grieved and quenched when the Corinthian saints were attaching themselves to party leaders, and refusing the ministry of the Spirit, because the channel used was not one favoured by them. In the confusion of Christendom today how much is the Spirit grieved, quenched and set aside by man's organization.

PRAYER IS BY THE SPIRIT

We read,

> "Praying always with all prayer and supplication *in the Spirit*, being watchful to this end with all perseverance and supplication for all the saints" (Ephesians 6:18).

The Apostle Jude writes,

> "But you, beloved, building yourselves up on your most holy faith, *praying in the Holy Spirit*, keep yourselves in the love of God, looking for the mercy of our Lord Jesus Christ unto eternal life" (Jude 20-21).

It is very clear from these Scriptures that prayer, true prayer, is in the Spirit. We may well search our hearts as to how far we do really pray. The Holy Spirit is gracious, and ever seeks to help us in our weakness when we approach the throne of grace with our petitions.

> "Likewise the Spirit also helps in our weaknesses. For we do not know what we should pray for as we ought, but the Spirit Himself makes intercession for us with groanings which cannot be uttered" (Romans 8:26).

This is a most wonderful and encouraging Scripture, showing that the Holy Spirit takes note of our weaknesses and infirmities, and renders us due help. What a wonderful partnership, and how strong is the help rendered when it is described as "groanings which cannot be uttered."

WORSHIP IS BY THE SPIRIT

We read,

> "The true worshippers will worship the Father *in spirit and truth*; for the Father is seeking such to worship Him. God is a Spirit, and those who worship Him must worship *in spirit and truth*" (John 4:23-24).

*   *   *   *   *

> "We are the circumcision, who worship God *in the Spirit*, rejoice in Christ Jesus, and have no confidence in the flesh" (Philippians 3:3).

Worship is the highest privilege the creature has. It will be the occupation of Heaven, and it is the happy privilege of the believer even here on earth.

DIVINE INTELLIGENCE IS BY THE SPIRIT

We read,

> "No one knows the things of God *except the Spirit of God*. Now we have received, not the spirit of the world, but the Spirit who is from God, that we might know the things that have been freely given to us by God. These things we also speak, not in words which man's wisdom teaches but which the Holy Spirit teaches, comparing spiritual things with spiritual" (1 Corinthians 2:11-13).

This Scripture is so plain in its meaning that it needs no explanation.

THE HOLY SPIRIT ONCE GIVEN IS NEVER WITHDRAWN

We read,

> "Do not grieve the Holy Spirit of God, by whom
> you were *sealed for the day of redemption*" (Ephesians
> 4:30).

This is a very clear passage. If the believer could grieve the
Spirit of God, so that He must withdraw His presence
from the believer, here is the place to state the possibility.
On the contrary, there is no such warning. The positive
statement is given that the sealing is "for the day of
redemption", that is, until the day comes when the Lord
at His second coming will translate His church to glory.

We read,

> "The gifts and the calling of God are irrevocable"
> (Romans 11:29),

that is to say that God will never change His mind, and
withdraw any gift He gives, or calling He makes. When
God gives a gift, or makes a calling, He never withdraws
His bounty. So it is with the gift of the Spirit of God.
Once given it is never withdrawn.

Typically, in the consecration of Aaron and his sons, we
find the oil (typical of the Holy Spirit) was put upon the
blood (typical of the atoning sacrifice of Christ applied in
all its holy effectiveness). This is the reason why the Spirit
is never withdrawn, because the indwelling is secured on
the righteous ground of the finished atoning work of our
Lord on the cross. All glory to His blessed name!

THE FRUIT OF THE SPIRIT

The believer, living in the Spirit, should walk in the Spirit,
and exhibit the fruit of the Spirit, which is

"Love, joy, peace, long-suffering, kindness, goodness, faithfulness, gentleness, self-control. Against such there is no law" (Galatians 5:22-23).

Fruit is not grown by effort. It is the result of nature in a suitable environment and under suitable conditions. So it is with the fruit of the Spirit. The first mark is love, divine love. That is the very nature of God, and should mark His children, who are partakers of the divine nature. No wonder where there is love and joy there is peace—peace in our hearts and ways. But we are sure to meet trying saints (perhaps we are trying ourselves), and we need to exercise long-suffering. Suffering not once or twice, but LONG-suffering. This is not natural to the flesh, but will be seen where the new nature is active within us. Faith, too, comes in. We walk by faith and not by sight. Faith gives us new adjustments, new visions, a new goal to reach, a new motivation. Faith for the Christian is more real than sight. Death may end our earthly journey in a moment, and sight is gone, but there can be no cessation to eternal life. Meek we need to be. Slow to take offence, as to give it. Lastly we need temperance, self-restraint, in all things, the keeping of the flesh in the place of death.

The Holy Spirit in relation to the One Body

We have been considering the Holy Spirit's indwelling in relation to the individual believer. Now we come to a very important aspect of the gift of the Holy Spirit: His coming into this world to form Christian fellowship. The Holy Spirit is the connection between Heaven and earth, between the believer and his Lord, and between believer and believer.

The day of Pentecost, and the descent of the Holy Spirit of God upon each of the assembled disciples at Jerusalem, was the hour of the Church's birth. A new era had set in. No longer was our Lord upon earth. Henceforth He was to be represented on earth by His people, as endued with power from on high in the gift of the Holy Spirit.

We read,

> "By one Spirit we were all baptized into one body—whether Jews or Greeks, whether slaves or free—and have all been made to drink into one Spirit" (1 Corinthians 12:13).

That is the believer's side of it. As to the heavenly side we read,

"And He [*the Lord Jesus*] is the Head of the body, the church, who is the Beginning, the First-born from the dead, that in all things He may have the pre-eminence" (Colossians 1:18).

*   *   *   *   *

"[God] put all things under His feet, and gave Him to be Head over all things to the church, which is His body, the fullness of Him who fills all in all" (Ephesians 1:22-23).

What a marvellous conception is this! The Apostle Paul having unfolded the gospel of the grace of God in the Epistle to the Romans, for one moment touches that which is about to engage our attention. He speaks of it as

"The revelation of the mystery which was kept secret since the world began but now has been made manifest, and by the prophetic Scriptures has been made known to all nations, according to the commandment of the everlasting God, for obedience to the faith" (Romans 16:25-26).

Again addressing the Ephesian church, he writes,

"To make all people see what is the fellowship of the mystery, which from the beginning of the ages has been hidden in God who created all things through Jesus Christ" (Ephesians 3:9).

Scripture seems to labour to express itself, as if human language were not an adequate vehicle for the fullness and glory of the divine communications.

The Holy Spirit does not leave the believer to pursue his way merely as an individual blessed of God, and on his way to glory, but by the Spirit the believer is united to

65

Christ in glory, and to each fellow-believer as members of the same body.

Christians form a fellowship the like of which can be seen nowhere else. It is a Divine fellowship. All human fellowships cease with time. This fellowship alone goes on into glory. It knows no frontiers. It knows no special language. It knows no social distinctions. It transcends everything of earth, and in the glorious light of this fellowship, earthly distinctions vanish, and believers of every clime, of every colour, of all ages and stages, form one Christian fellowship. There is only one Divine fellowship seen in the New Testament, only one ransomed church of God, and it is by the Holy Spirit this comes about.

The writer was once at the breaking of bread in the United States of America. There were present Americans, English, Scots, Irish, Germans, French, Swedes, Russians and Jews. And yet we were one in Christ, the Holy Spirit indwelt each believer, each was a member of the one body. Christ was our Head in the glory.

> "There is one body and one Spirit, just as you were called in one hope of your calling" (Ephesians 4:4).

It is well to note that the expression, one body, is used as a simile to express the closest, the most intimate fellowship. Can anything in nature be closer in action than the members of one's natural body? So with the mystic body of Christ. The expression is employed to set forth the closest communion possible.

But please note how this comes about:

> "There is one body and ONE SPIRIT" (Ephesians 4:4).

There are some who emphasize, "There is one body", but forget to realize how utterly dependent the concept of the one body is upon the indwelling Holy Spirit of God. Even nature illustrates this when we read,

"The body without the spirit is dead" (James 2:26).

No wonder when Christians insist on the one body, and forget the one Spirit, the whole thing becomes in their hands a dead ecclesiasticism. It is a most withering thing, and has wrought untold mischief in the church of God. With the extreme assumption of being the only custodians of the truth, and affecting to despise all other Christians, such will shrink in their narrow-mindedness the one body down to the limit of their own little fragment. Professing loudly to be the only Christians on earth to be maintaining the truth of the one body, they attribute to their own little circle that which is true of all Christians, and become the most sectarian of the sectarian.

There is one body. Emphasize that, but don't forget, the whole secret of the one body lies in the fact that the Holy Spirit indwells each believer. If that is grasped, what happy practical results there would be.

Psalm 133:1-2 affords a beautiful illustration of this:

"Behold, how good and how pleasant it is for brethren to dwell together in unity! It is like the precious oil upon the head, running down on the beard, the beard of Aaron, running down on the edge of his garments."

This illustrates a great truth, that divine unity only comes from the blessed glorious Head in Heaven, even our Lord Jesus Christ. If only God's people would grasp this, how blessed it would be. Aaron, the high priest, in the psalm is typical of our Lord. Ointment is typical of the Holy Spirit. The ointment descended from Aaron's head. Does this not illustrate how the Holy Spirit was sent down from our blessed risen glorified Lord, our great Head in Heaven. From Aaron's head the ointment flowed down to his beard. This may set forth the very important result of the companying of the apostles with our Lord during His earthly ministry. By this their minds were formed. Our Lord specially spoke much to them during His last few days on earth of the coming of the Holy Spirit. The new dispensation was being prepared. Christianity was to be established. So the Apostles were brought into a fellowship, that of the Father and His Son, Jesus Christ. Then the precious ointment ran down Aaron's garment. Does this not illustrate how the apostles in their turn declared their fellowship to the disciples, so that Christian fellowship might widen out to take in all God's people, down to the feeblest member of the body of Christ?

The Apostle John, identifying the other apostles as witnesses with him, writes,

> "That which we have seen and heard we declare to you, that you also may have fellowship with us; and truly our fellowship is with the Father and with His Son Jesus Christ. And these things we write to you that your joy may be full" (1 John 1:3-4).

So the influence of the Holy Spirit is to descend to the youngest and feeblest member of the body of Christ. The line of a verse comes to one's mind as appropriate,

"Good for the feeblest heart."

We remember vividly an exhortation from an old brother, who did not set out to be a teacher, but on this particular occasion, over half a century ago, he uttered a striking truth, to which we should all do well to pay heed. He said, "Brethren, hold the Head in Heaven. If you don't hold the Head in Heaven, you won't hold each other on earth." How pithy, and as true as it is pithy. Remember, we are never exhorted in Scripture to keep the unity of the one body. "There IS one body." We cannot make it, or break it. But we are exhorted to keep *the unity of the SPIRIT*. We are exhorted to

> "Lead a life worthy of the calling with which you were called, with all lowliness and gentleness, with long-suffering, bearing with one another in love, endeavouring to keep *the unity OF THE SPIRIT in the bond of peace*" (Ephesians 4:1-3).

If this were our aim and object how happy it would be. It is very edifying to see men and women of different characters naturally, of different ages, of different social positions, all coming under the influence of the Spirit of God, and happy unity resulting.

It is by the Spirit that the Head in Heaven directs and sustains His members on earth, in order that His life may be reproduced in them.

We once heard it said of saints who were endeavouring to keep the unity of the Spirit in the bond of peace, that they had strong arms and legs, but no head. Their endeavour did not mean liberty to fraternize with any and every Christian in whatever ecclesiastical association they might chance to be, but their aim was to follow closely the instruction of the Spirit of God as set forth in the Scriptures for the guidance of God's people. The Roman Catholic Church looks up to a head in Rome. The Church of England looks up to a spiritual head in Canterbury. Other bodies have their heads, called president, moderator, etc.

But these people, they said, had no head. The answer was very obvious: there could be no strong arms and legs, if there were no head. Strong arms and legs prove a sound and healthy head. To see the Head these saints acknowledged, you would have to look past Rome or Canterbury, etc., *and look up to Heaven,* and see by faith the *only* Head that Scripture acknowledges, even our blessed Lord and Saviour, Jesus Christ.

It is true that Scripture tacitly admits that we shall meet with difficulties in this fellowship. The flesh will creep in, and we know that Satan is full of wiles, and would lead Christians astray, if he can. So Scripture in this connection exhorts us to be long-suffering, to forbear one another in love, to be marked by lowliness and meekness. There is plenty of scope for the exercise of these qualities.

One thing is certain, that if we each seek to be governed by the Spirit, each of us holding the Head, that is in living vital touch with the Lord, answering to His guidance, very happy results will show themselves.

The Holy Spirit in the Book of the Revelation

The writer of the Book of the Revelation, the beloved aged Apostle John, alludes several times to the seven Spirits of God:

"The seven Spirits who are before His throne" (Revelation 1:4).

*   *   *   *   *

"These things says He who has the seven Spirits of God and the seven stars" (Revelation 3:1).

*   *   *   *   *

"There were seven lamps of fire burning before the throne, which are the seven Spirits of God" (Revelation 4:5).

*   *   *   *   *

"Stood a Lamb as though it had been slain, having seven horns and seven eyes, which are the seven Spirits of God sent out into all the earth" (Revelation 5:6).

The question is often asked, Are there seven Spirits of God? The answer is, that there is only one Holy Spirit of God. The symbol of the seven Spirits is to set forth the varied activities of the Holy Spirit.

An illustration may help. The golden candlestick in the Tabernacle was one candlestick, yet it was made up of seven stems each carrying a lamp. You might speak of the one candlestick or lampstand on one occasion, or of the seven lamps on another occasion. In both cases you would be correct.

Isaiah 11:1-2, may further illustrate,

> "There shall come forth a Rod from the stem of Jesse, and a Branch shall grow out of his roots. The Spirit of the LORD shall rest upon Him, the Spirit of wisdom and understanding, the Spirit of counsel and might, the Spirit of knowledge and of the fear of the LORD."

One Spirit, but seen in different aspects.

The Spirit of God as seen in the Book of the Revelation is active in judgment, first in the church of God, and then in the world. When our Lord is seen walking in the midst of the seven golden candlesticks, it is a figurative way of stating that our Lord reviews His church in its various phases, and passes judgment upon that which is not of Himself. Seven times over we read,

> "He who has an ear, let him hear what the Spirit says to the churches" (Revelation 2:7, 11, 17, 29; 3:6, 13, 22).

When the present Church period, indicated by the seven Churches of Revelation 2 and 3, expires, judgment will branch out into the world. We read,

"For the time has come for judgment to begin at the house of God; and if it begins with us first, what will be the end of those who do not obey the gospel of God?" (1 Peter 4:17).

Two Scriptures plainly show how the Holy Spirit of God will be active in judgment when the church period is over.

"And from the throne proceeded lightnings, thunderings, and voices. And there were seven lamps of fire burning before the throne, which are *the seven Spirits of God*" (Revelation 4:5).

*　　*　　*　　*　　*

"And I looked, and behold, in the midst of the throne and of the four living creatures, and in the midst of the elders, stood a Lamb as though it had been slain, having seven horns and seven eyes, which are *the seven Spirits of God* sent out into all the earth" (Revelation 5:6).

Seven lamps burning before the throne are symbolic of the intensity of the Holy Spirit's action in judgment in this world. The throne speaks of immutable and irresistible power. The seven horns speak of *active* judgment (see for illustration what is said of horns in Daniel 8). Seven eyes speak of full discrimination. These are identified with the Lamb, the Lord Jesus, and as fully identified with the Holy Spirit, showing the wonderful blending of Divine Persons in purpose, will and power.

The Spirit, too, is the power by which the Revelation of "the things which are, and the things which will take place after this" (Revelation 1:19) is given. The Apostle John was

"*In the Spirit* on the Lord's day" (Revelation 1:10),

when this wonderful vision was unfolded to him.

Then, when he was caught up in vision to Heaven to be shown "the things which will take place after this", we read again,

> "Immediately I was *in the Spirit*; and behold, a throne set in Heaven, and One sat on the throne" (Revelation 4:2).

Finally, when he had the vision of the holy city, the New Jerusalem descending out of Heaven from God, the presentation of the Church in display and administration in the coming millennial age, we read,

> "And he carried me away *in the Spirit* to a great and high mountain, and showed me the great city, the holy Jerusalem, descending out of Heaven from God" (Revelation 21:10).

The last mention of the Holy Spirit in the Scriptures is very beautiful:

> "And *the Spirit* and the bride say, 'Come!' And let him who hears say, 'Come!' And let him who thirsts come. Whoever desires, let him take the water of life freely" (Revelation 22:17).

It is sweet to see the journey nearly finished, the church's pilgrimage almost ended, and the Spirit saying to the Lord to come and take His own to be with Him for ever; the church, by the Spirit, joining in with deep affection. Sweet it is to see the evangelistic touch at the very last, the Spirit of God yearning over the lost sons of men, seeking their eternal blessing.

The Bible begins with the Spirit of God hovering over the face of the waters, and ends with the invitation for the thirsty to drink of the water of life.

What a wonderful place from start to finish has the Spirit of God, One with the Father and the Son in the unity of the Godhead.

> *"Father, Son and Holy Spirit—*
> *Three in One! We give Thee praise!*
> *For the riches we inherit*
> *Heart and voice to Thee we raise!*
> *We adore Thee! We adore Thee!"*

George West Frazer (1830-1896)

Part 2: The Great Adversary

Satan is a pure Hebrew word, meaning Adversary. It is an ordinary word to designate a person who stands in opposition. In Scripture, it is specially used to designate the fallen spiritual being, commonly called the Devil. In this latter sense we give this sketch of his being, character, and activities.

Satan's being

The first mention of the name, Satan, in the Old Testament is found in 1 Chronicles 21:1,

"Now Satan stood up against Israel, and moved David to number Israel."

Satan is mentioned fourteen times in Job 1 and 2. There is one mention in the Psalms:

"Set a wicked man over him, and let an accuser [Hebrew: *Satan*; the adversary, N.Tr.] stand at his right hand" (Psalm 109:6).

Finally, the prophet, Zechariah, in a vision sees Satan standing at the right hand of the Angel of the LORD. We read:

"And the LORD said to Satan, 'The LORD rebuke you, Satan! The LORD who has chosen Jerusalem rebuke you! Is this not a brand plucked from the fire?'" (Zechariah 3:2).

These are the only instances where the name, Satan, occurs in the whole of the Old Testament.

The word *adversary*, as referring to Satan, occurs in the New Testament in a passage which may come to the mind of the reader:

> "Your adversary the Devil walks about like a roaring lion, seeking whom he may devour" (1 Peter 5:8).

The word translated *adversary* in the above passage is the Greek word, *antidikos*, which is used to designate an opponent in a lawsuit. It is used to set forth the implacable nature of Satan as opposed to God, and His people, and His interests in this world. The word, *Devil*, is only found in the New Testament.

Despite the fewness of times that Satan, the Adversary, is mentioned in the Old Testament, there is no doubt but that he is the active agent behind the scenes. That Satan should provoke David to commit an evil act in numbering Israel shows how he is behind all the evil in the world.

WHAT IS THE ORIGIN OF SATAN?

The fullest light on this mysterious subject is presented to us in highly symbolical language in Ezekiel 28, where we read of the Prince of Tyre and the King of Tyre, the latter very definitely being a description of Satan, the former his human understudy. Satan ever seeks expression through human agents, hence the connection between the Prince of Tyre and the King of Tyre in this chapter. Any agent of Satan is marked by possessing the same traits that mark Satan himself.

So we find the Prince of Tyre using very extravagant blasphemous language. This is seen in the rebuke administered to him:

> "Because your heart is lifted up, and you say, 'I am a god, I sit in the seat of gods, in the midst of the

seas,' yet you are a man, and not a god, though you set your heart as the heart of a god" (Ezekiel 28:2).

This is what Satan aimed at, to be God, and sit in the place of supreme power, and this is what his human understudy aims at.

The language the Prince of Tyre used reminds us of the pretentions of Adolph Hitler in the mid-20th century. He too regarded himself as a man of destiny, and he was almost, if not quite, regarded as a god. One could not understand his phenomenal meteoric rise to such immense power and success apart from satanic power. His schemes were too grandiose for any human mind.

In India, the author met a doctor, the daughter of a Polish rabbi, a strong character, and an earnest Christian. She loathed Hitler and all his works. Yet she told the author that when in Berlin she heard him three or four times. She would begin by feeling very antipathetic, but before long she would be swept off her feet by some weird supernatural power, and could not release herself from this malign power as long as she was in his presence. For the first three or four minutes he would speak like an ordinary man, and then his face would take on a different and terrible look, and in an instant the audience would be gripped by a power which she and many others believed to be satanic.

It is worth recounting this experience as illustrating the link between the Prince of Tyre and the King of Tyre (Satan). The Prince of Tyre was clearly a man. The divine judgment upon him was that he should "die the death of the uncircumcised by the hand of aliens" (Ezekiel 28:10).

But when we come to the description of the origin of the King of Tyre, we can only come to the conclusion that it describes the origin of Satan himself.

> "You were the seal of perfection, full of wisdom and perfect in beauty. You were in Eden, the garden of God; every precious stone was your covering: the sardius, topaz, and diamond, beryl, onyx, and jasper, sapphire, turquoise, and emerald with gold. The workmanship of your timbrels and pipes was prepared for you on the day you were created" (Ezekiel 28:12-13).

This is a highly symbolic description of a creation of wondrous power and beauty. Timbrels and pipes (flutes)—musical instruments commonly used in the East at weddings and feasts—show this creature was created to utter God's praises. Note, too, how the precious stones are more or less identical with the gems that glittered on the high priest's breastplate (Exodus 28:17-21).

Then we are told he was "the anointed cherub who covers", that is, that defends, a word used for the cherubim covering the mercy seat. He walked upon the holy mount of God. He was perfect in all his ways till iniquity was found in him.

> "Your heart was lifted up because of your beauty; you corrupted your wisdom for the sake of your splendour; I cast you to the ground, I laid you before kings, that they might gaze at you" (Ezekiel 28:17).

Could this be a description of anything but the fall of Satan? He was evidently the highest creature that God in His wisdom created. Alas! pride was his ruin, and pride is designated in Scripture as

"The same condemnation as the Devil" (1 Timothy 3:6).

Our Lord described him as a murderer and liar:

> "You are of your father the Devil, and the desires of your father you want to do. He was a murderer from the beginning, and does not stand in the truth, because there is no truth in him. When he speaks a lie, he speaks from his own resources, for he is a liar and the father of it" (John 8:44).

This then, we believe, is the Scripture revelation to us of the origin of Satan, and his fall. The details are few and scanty, but what we do know is very impressive and awe-inspiring. For such a wonderful creation of God to fall from his high estate, carrying with him a mighty following of angels, is terrible to contemplate.

We shall see now how Satan's own temptation and fall determined the manner of his approach to our first parents, and even to our Lord Himself when he dared to tempt Him.

Satan and the fall of man

SATAN'S TEMPTATION OF OUR FIRST PARENTS

When this earth was ready for man's creation and residence, sin was already in God's universe. Here was Satan's chance to oppose God. He approached our first parents under the guise of a serpent. We have Scripture warrant for identifying the serpent in the narrative as Satan. We read:

> "So the great Dragon was cast out, *that Serpent of old*, called the Devil and Satan, who deceives the whole world" (Revelation 12:9).

* * * * *

> "He laid hold of the Dragon, *that Serpent of old*, who is the Devil and Satan, and bound him for a thousand years" (Revelation 20:2).

* * * * *

> "I fear, lest somehow, as *the Serpent* deceived Eve by his craftiness, so your minds may be corrupted from the simplicity that is in Christ" (2 Corinthians 11:3).

Many think that the serpent as originally created by God was a beautiful creature with an erect carriage, and able to express itself in language. Whether it be so, or not, whether speech was the serpent's, or Satan's in possession of the body of the serpent for his own purposes, we cannot say, but it is clear that the approach to Eve did not terrify her as anything unusual. Up to then, no sin had come into God's fair creation. Creatures were then in all the innocence and grace of sinless creation. We gather this must have been so when we are told that the fall of man involved the fall of creation.

> "The creation was subjected to futility, not willingly, but because of Him who subjected it in hope" (Romans 8:20).

Thank God, it is not always to be so, for the Scripture goes on to say in view of the coming of our Lord to reign upon the earth,

> "The creation itself also will be delivered from the bondage of corruption into the glorious liberty of the children of God" (verse 21).

In that day, our Lord says,

> "I will rejoice in Jerusalem, and joy in My people; the voice of weeping shall no longer be heard in her, nor the voice of crying. ... The wolf and the lamb shall feed together, the lion shall eat straw like the ox, and dust shall be the serpent's food. They shall not hurt nor destroy in all My holy mountain" (Isaiah 65:19-25).

We are told that the serpent was more cunning than any beast of the field. We must attribute this craftiness to Satan, who may have possessed the body of the serpent, and controlled its actions and speech.

THE TEMPTATION IN THE GARDEN OF EDEN

Satan, finding Eve by herself, began by insinuating that God was not altogether good to His creatures,

> "Has God indeed said, 'You shall not eat of every tree of the garden'?" (Genesis 3:1).

God had given every tree of the garden for food save one solitary tree. This prohibition was a test of the creature's obedience to the Creator. Moreover, the Creator knew that if they did eat of the tree of knowledge of good and evil, the result would be the ruin of man's innocence, the poisoning of his very system by the introduction of the knowledge of evil, with no power to resist it. Therefore, His prohibition was merciful. Satan, too, knew that to eat of the fruit of the tree of knowledge of good and evil would mean the ruin and fall of God's creatures. How evil was the great Adversary to deliberately work such havoc and ruin. No one can faintly realize the awful tide of sin and wickedness that had its germ in this one act of disobedience.

When Eve responded, and told Satan that this one tree was forbidden, and that the penalty for eating of it would be death, Satan, the liar and father of lies, told the cruellest of lies when he assured her,

> "You will not surely die. For God knows that in the day you eat it your eyes will be opened, and you will be like God, knowing good and evil" (Genesis 3:4-5)

"You will be like God": Satan dangled the same bait that had brought about his own downfall. In the desire to rise out of the position in which God had placed His creature lies the secret of the fall.

Moreover, the tree was attractive from three points of view. It was good for food. It was pleasant to the eyes. It was desired to make the eater wise. Thus entered into the world the terrible system of lawlessness and iniquity.

> "For all that is in the world—the lust of the flesh, the lust of the eyes, and the pride of life—is not of the Father but is of the world" (1 John 2:16).

There is nothing wrong to desire good food, given by a beneficent Creator for the sustenance of man. But when there were many trees able to satisfy, why eat of one hedged round by God's expressed prohibition? To eat of the tree in those circumstances meant "the lust of the flesh". Neither is it wrong to admire what is pleasant to the eyes. God, who created beauty, must rejoice when His creature appreciates what is beautiful. But when this admiration is so strong as to lead to taking what God has forbidden, it becomes a grievous thing—"the lust of the eyes". The third character of the temptation, "the pride of life", was the strongest of all. To be "like God, knowing good and evil", surely that was worth risking the eating of the tree in defiance of God's prohibition, and risking the sentence of death in all its horrors.

Under this threefold temptation, Eve committed the terrible act of putting out her hand and taking of the forbidden fruit. Little did she realize the results that would flow from her act, stretching down to the appalling state of things we see in the world today.

> "Adam was not deceived, but the woman being deceived, fell into transgression" (1 Timothy 2:14).

Eve gave of the forbidden fruit to Adam; and he, not being deceived, was all the more culpable as head to the woman, and thus shared in the fall.

87

"Through one man sin entered the world, and death through sin, and thus death spread to all men, because all sinned" (Romans 5:12).

Satan thus obtained an unholy triumph over the very first pair in this world.

Satan's temptation of the Lord

Centuries went by, and Satan, flushed with an unbroken series of victories over fallen man, at last attempted his most daring assault—upon the Son of God. At the beginning of our Lord's earthly ministry we read:

> "Then Jesus was led up by the Spirit into the wilderness to be tempted by the Devil. And when He had fasted forty days and forty nights, afterwards He was hungry" (Matthew 4:1-2).

It was fitting that our adorable Lord, as the dependent Man, should undergo this temptation. Hence He was led of the Spirit into the wilderness. The circumstances in which the temptation took place stand in vivid contrast to those in the Garden of Eden. Our first parents were in a beautiful garden with plenty of luscious fruit with which to satisfy their hunger. Only *one* tree was withheld from them in God's mercy. Our Lord was in a wilderness, had fasted for forty days, was hungry, and amid wild beasts.

Satan's first temptation appealed to "the lust of the flesh". To his utter surprise he found no response to this in our

Lord. He was sinless, and there was nothing in Him to answer to the evil externally. The Devil said,

> "If You are the Son of God, command that these stones become bread" (Matthew 4:3).

Our Lord, as the dependent Man, answered, quoting Scripture:

> "It is written, 'Man shall not live by bread alone, but by every word that proceeds from the mouth of God'" (Matthew 4:4).

What a sharp contrast to the conduct of Eve! Our Lord would live by *every* word that issued from the mouth of God. If Eve had done that she might have been living today. Alas! she contravened what God said as to the tree of the knowledge of good and evil. Our Lord, on the contrary, would not take Himself out of the hand of God, and perform a miracle at the bidding of Satan. The sword of the Spirit was His defence and with it He foiled the enemy.

Again the attack was pressed home. Satan this time took our Lord into the holy city, and set Him on a pinnacle of the Temple. He said to Him:

> "If You are the Son of God, throw Yourself down. For it is written: 'He shall give His angels charge concerning You,' and, 'In their hands they shall bear You up, lest You dash Your foot against a stone'" (Matthew 4:6).

This temptation appealed to "the pride of life". And never is the Devil more cunning than when he quotes Scripture. To add to, or take from, the Word of God is very serious. Turn to Psalm 91:11-12, and you will see that Satan designedly, and for his own evil ends, left out words, which we draw attention to by printing them in italics.

"For He shall give His angels charge over You, to keep You *in all YOUR ways*" (Psalm 91:11-12).

Satan demanded of our Lord that He should prove He was the Son of God by walking *in Satan's way*. Our Lord's way was that of absolute obedience to the will of God, and in that He was safe. Again our Lord took up the sword of the Spirit:

"Jesus said to him, 'It is written again, "You shall not tempt the LORD your God"'" (Matthew 4:7).

Our Lord quoted Scripture, but in His blessed hands, it was the sword of the Spirit.

Foiled again, Satan made a third attempt. He took our Lord into an exceedingly high mountain, and showed him all the kingdoms of the world, and their glory,

"And he said to Him, 'All these things I will give You if You will fall down and worship me'" (Matthew 4:9).

Here Satan disclosed what is in his heart of hearts. He fell, seeking to be God, and carrying with him in his fall angels who shared in his rebellion. Here again he seeks worship, and awful to say, worship from the Son of God. Here he tries "the lust of the eyes". What a sight it must have been, the kingdoms of this world and their glory, all stretched out before His gaze. Our Lord was proof against this last temptation, and again He used the sword of the Spirit, saying,

"Away with you, Satan! For it is written, 'You shall worship the LORD your God, and Him only you shall serve'" (Matthew 4:10).

Worship belongs only to God. What a profound and unthinkable degradation it would have been to have worshipped the Devil, the very arch-enemy of God. How terrible was the temptation! How acutely our adorable Lord must have suffered in its presentation. At last the Devil left Him, and angels ministered to Him.

For the first time in all his long history of wicked rebellion against God, the Devil had come up against One in whom he could find no response whatever.

So where our first parents failed, our Lord triumphed. If He had not triumphed, there would have been the collapse of His whole mission to this world. He could not have been our Saviour. How we rejoice in His holy triumph over the great Adversary.

Again the Devil assailed our Lord at the end of His earthly life when all the dread ordeal of the cross was before Him. The Devil utterly failed again. Our Lord could say,

> "I will no longer talk much with you, for the ruler of this world is coming, and he has nothing in Me" (John 14:30).

Satan's aspirations

GOD THE SUPREME RULER AND SOLE OBJECT OF WORSHIP

There are two things, among many, that exclusively belong to God. He is the only supreme Ruler of the universe. He is the only right Object of worship. Satan dared to aspire to these two things. There are two descriptions in the Word of God, which answer to Satan's aspirations in these directions.

"Now *the RULER of this world* will be cast out" (John 12:31).

* * * * *

"*The RULER of this world* is coming" (John 14:30).

* * * * *

"Whose minds *the GOD of this age* has blinded, who do not believe" (2 Corinthians 4:4).

It is sadly interesting to see that in the last days Satan will seek to get universal dominion in this world through the Beast, the Head of the revived Roman Empire; and gratify his desire for worship through the Antichrist, the man of sin. Satan can only express himself through agents. We are reminded again of the Prince of Tyre and the King of Tyre.

There have always sprung up men in this world who have aimed at universal dominion. One can only come to the conclusion that behind these attempts there is Satan seeking to gratify his lust for power through human agents. See Alexander the Great, who wept because there were no more worlds to conquer; Julius Caesar, who sought to make the Roman Empire the mistress of the world; the great Napoleon, who overran many countries in his time; in the author's own lifetime, Adolph Hitler, whose meteoric career was the wonder of the world. Openly he sought the aid of spiritism. Many firmly believed he was possessed of an evil spirit. It would be good if Christians were more aware of the might and craftiness of Satan, and of his ceaseless schemes for the furtherance of the destruction of mankind, body and soul.

SATAN IS CALLED THE RULER OF THE DEMONS

We read,

> "The Pharisees said, 'He casts out demons by *the ruler of the demons*'" (Matthew 9:34).

*   *   *   *   *

> "When the Pharisees heard it they said, 'This fellow does not cast out demons except by Beelzebub, *the ruler of the demons*'" (Matthew 12:24).

The word *demon* in these verses, referring to a fallen spiritual being other than the Devil himself, is incorrectly translated *devil* in the Authorized Version. The Greek word for the Devil is *diabolos*, the accuser, slanderer. The word for fallen spiritual being other than the Devil is *daimon*, a deified spirit, but in the Bible standing for Satan's fallen followers, often called in the Gospels unclean spirits because of their power to pollute the minds and bodies of mankind.

These verses bring us to the consideration of the statement made previously that Satan when he fell carried with him a vast number of adherents. Evidently this was well recognized by the Pharisees, and is supported by Scripture itself. Scripture indicates that there are two classes of fallen spiritual beings, whose fortunes are linked up with Satan, their leader and head. One class is described to us in Jude 6:

> "The angels who did not keep their proper domain, but left their own habitation, He has reserved in everlasting chains under darkness for the judgment of the great day."

Evidently this class can have no power to tempt mankind, nor can it be under the control of Satan. They must have sinned in an especially outrageous way, leading to the fate of being kept in darkness in everlasting chains.

There is another class of fallen angels, in Scripture called demons, who evidently are allowed a range of activity in this world. We have ample proof of this in the four Gospels. That these unclean spirits have the power to enter and possess the bodies of men and animals is evident. We read:

> "Now there was a man in their synagogue with an unclean spirit. And he cried out, saying, 'Let us alone! What have we to do with You, Jesus of Nazareth? Did You come to destroy us? I know who You are—the Holy One of God!'" (Mark 1:23-24).

$*$ $*$ $*$ $*$ $*$

> "And all the demons begged Him, saying, 'Send us to the swine, that we may enter them.' And at once Jesus gave them permission. Then the unclean spirits went out and entered the swine (there were

about two thousand); and the herd ran violently down the steep place into the sea, and drowned in the sea" (Mark 5:12-13).

*   *   *   *   *

"Mary called Magdalene, out of whom had come seven demons" (Luke 8:2).

These demons are often designated as "unclean spirits", for it has ever been Satan's aim to pollute men's minds to destroy their souls, and to bring about evil diseases to destroy their bodies. That these hordes of evil spirits are highly organized we gather from Scripture.

"And they had as king over them the angel of the bottomless pit, whose name in Hebrew is Abaddon, but in Greek he has the name Apollyon [*destroyer*]" (Revelation 9:11).

A king is no king unless he has subjects, who form under his rule a kingdom. That the underworld is highly organized is here plainly stated. Other Scriptures support this view. In Daniel 10:20 the Prince of Persia, and the Prince of Greece, fallen demons evidently, are referred to as two agents of the satanic underworld, put in charge of Satan's interests in those countries. They stand in opposition to Michael, the Archangel of God, who Scripture states is put in charge of God's interests in connection with the children of Israel. These little peeps into the underworld show how highly organized are the forces of evil in this world.

Satan and the Last Days

WHAT IS THE BOTTOMLESS PIT?

This title is only found in the Book of the Revelation. It would be better translated by the word *abyss*, a very deep place. It must be carefully distinguished from Hell. It has a king, Satan, called "the angel of the bottomless pit". Though it has a king he is not complete master, for the abyss has a key over which Heaven has power, showing that entry and exit is not unlimited. Satan will be bound in it for the thousand years of the millennial reign of our Lord on this earth. It is clear that God can and does restrain as well as allow demon activity. We read:

> "And now you know what is restraining, that he may be revealed in his own time. For the mystery of lawlessness is already at work; only He who now restrains will do so until He is taken out of the way. And then the Lawless One will be revealed [*Antichrist*], whom the Lord will consume with the breath of His mouth and destroy with the brightness of His coming" (2 Thessalonians 2:6-8).

That God will allow a terrible eruption of demon power to ascend out of the bottomless pit in the last days is seen in Revelation 9. Its description is couched in very colourful and symbolic language.

In the days when the fifth angel shall sound his trumpet of doom, a falling star (a great dignitary, who apostatizes from truth, and who sells himself to the Devil) will have the key of the bottomless pit given to him.

> "And he opened the bottomless pit, and smoke arose out of the pit like the smoke of a great furnace. And the sun and the air were darkened because of the smoke of the pit" (Revelation 9:2).

Out of this smoke came locusts, symbolical of spiritual forces, evil spirits, let loose for their work of malevolence. They were like horses prepared for battle, that is, prepared for powerful concerted action. On their heads were crowns of gold, speaking of previous victories, just as soldiers may have a row of medals. They have faces as of men, showing intelligence, but accompanied by subjection and effeminacy, for they had hair like women. They were ferocious for they have teeth like lions. Breastplates of iron sets forth invulnerability when attacked. They have stings like scorpions, speaking of the form of trial they are capable of inflicting, even the instilling of untruth of such a nature as to produce intolerable anguish of spirit, making life unbearable and leading to utter despair.

This gives us a little idea of what tremendous power Satan controls, as far as he is permitted to do so.

Spiritism will play a terrible part in the drama of the Last Days

That spiritism under the hand of Satan will have an overwhelming and sinister part to play in the last days is evident in what the Apostle Paul wrote to Timothy,

"The Spirit expressly says that in latter times some will depart from the faith, giving heed to deceiving spirits and doctrines of demons, speaking lies in hypocrisy, having their own conscience seared with a hot iron, forbidding to marry, and commanding to abstain from foods" (1 Timothy 4:1-3).

When evil spirits pretend to be the spirits of departed friends they speak "lies in hypocrisy". At the very bottom of this unclean system is the teaching of free love, that is "forbidding to marry", but to be free for any lustful alliance that may tempt man or woman. "To abstain from foods" is seen in the fact that mediums to be successful must refrain from animal food, and live on a vegetarian diet.

At the time of writing (1944), it was well known that Hitler had an ear for the occult, that he consulted mediums. He was said to neither smoke nor drink, nor did he eat meat. With his attack on the Christian religion, seeking to substitute for it the worship of Germany as the super-nation, and of himself as Führer, we can see how easily things may develop in fulfilment of prophecy concerning the end of the age.

This is very clearly seen in Revelation 16:13-14, where we read:

"And I saw three unclean spirits like frogs coming out of the mouth of the Dragon [*Satan*], out of the mouth of the Beast [*Head of the revived Roman Empire*], and out of the mouth of the False Prophet [*the Antichrist*]. For they are spirits of demons, performing signs, which go out to the kings of the earth and of the whole world, to gather them to the battle of that great day of God Almighty."

This is a passage to ponder over. Here we see indicated vast streams of satanic influence, embracing in their hypnotic power the kings of the earth and of the world, energizing them to one vast mighty effort to destroy God's people, for Armageddon is situated in the Holy Land. These will be dark days indeed, staggering our wildest imagination.

God does not bring evil into existence, but there are times in the history of the world when, in His wisdom and the carrying out and furtherance of His own plans, He withdraws His restraining hand, and allows evil to rear its head, so that it may be destroyed, and brought to nothing. For instance, God said to Pharaoh long ago,

> "But indeed for this purpose I have raised you up, that I may show My power in you, and that My name may be declared in all the earth" (Exodus 9:16).

Who shall question what God is pleased to restrain or what He allows to come into play?

Satan's activities

SATAN MOSTLY ACTS THROUGH HIS AGENTS

Rarely do we find it recorded in Scripture that Satan acts personally. He largely acts through his followers. However, when he acts personally, we find the occasion to be of special importance. He acted personally in the Garden of Eden, possessing the body of the serpent for the purpose of approaching our first parents. He acted personally in the temptation of our adorable Lord in the wilderness. Again he acted personally when he entered into the body of Judas Iscariot, so as to drive him to the awful act of treachery in betraying his Lord and Master for the greed of thirty paltry pieces of silver, furnished of all men by the chief priests. We shudder to think of Judas being possessed of the Devil himself. The greatest act of treachery in all time was enacted that day.

SATAN IS A FALLEN CREATURE

It is well to emphasize that Satan is not possessed of powers beyond creature range, though in his case his wonderful powers as "the covering cherub" have been sadly perverted to evil ends. Satan is neither omnipotent, omniscient, nor omnipresent. People often say lightly, The Devil tempted me. Did he? Possibly he did through his agents, but the Devil can only be in one place at once. Doubtless as king of the bottomless pit, his time must be largely taken with devising schemes and organizing his forces for evil. His kingdom is highly organized in deadly opposition to all that is of God and of Christ in this world.

The Apostle John bids us test the spirits. The test is, Do they believe that Jesus Christ is come in the flesh? If they fail in this test, they are not of God.

> "You are of God, little children, and have overcome them [*evil spiritual beings*], because He who is in you [*the indwelling Holy Spirit*] is greater than he who is in the world [*Satan*]" (1 John 4:4).

This is indeed heartening reading. The feeblest, youngest believer indwelt by the Spirit of God, has a power within him infinitely greater than that of the evil one. The might of the Holy Spirit is the power of God: infinite, resourceful, omnipotent. Christians are safe as they yield themselves to the Holy Spirit of God. Satan's wiles may be subtle, but God is behind everything, and the Christian has a wonderful resource in prayer.

GOD CAN USE SATAN FOR BLESSING

At first sight this may surprise some of our readers, but this is seen in a clear light in the Book of Job. Job was the greatest of the men of the East in his day. He was blameless and upright, feared God, and shunned evil. When Satan presented himself before the LORD, his attention was drawn to Job, the LORD speaking in praise of his being blameless and upright. Satan sneered that Job did not serve God for nothing, that if his circumstances were reversed, Job would curse God to His face.

God then gave Satan power over all that Job possessed.

In one day Job was stripped of property and children, as a man has never been, one might think, in all the history of the world. The Sabeans took 500 pairs of oxen and 500 female donkeys, killing all the servants in charge of them but one, who escaped to tell the sorrowful tale. Fire came down from heaven, and destroyed 7,000 sheep, and the servants in charge of them, and only one escaped to tell the awful news. Hard on his heels came a servant, who was the only survivor to escape, when the Chaldeans in three bands fell upon 3,000 camels, and took them away. From being the richest man in the East, Job was reduced to poverty in one short day.

But worse, infinitely worse was to come. Job had seven sons and three daughters, and that day they were feasting in their eldest brother's house, when a great wind struck the house, and it fell upon his seven sons and three daughters and destroyed them. Was there ever such a quick succession of devastating blows, the last worse than all the others put together?

What did Job do? He tore his robe, shaved his head, fell down to the ground and worshipped,

> "And he said: 'Naked I came from my mother's womb, and naked shall I return there. The LORD gave, and the LORD has taken away; blessed be the name of the LORD'" (Job 1:21).

One can only marvel at such a man. Was there ever such wonderful conduct in such circumstances?

Again there came a day when Satan presented himself to the LORD. God spoke to Satan of Job retaining his integrity, in spite of his awful experiences. Satan sneered that if God would only touch Job's body, there would be a different story to tell.

"Satan answered the LORD and said, 'Skin for skin!
Yes, all that a man has he will give for his life. But
stretch out Your hand now, and touch his bone and
his flesh, and he will surely curse You to Your face!'"
(Job 2:4-5).

God gave permission to Satan to deal with Job's body,
short of taking his life. At Satan's bidding, boils broke out
on Job from the sole of his foot to the crown of his head.
Can you imagine a more terrible plight? Stripped of
property and family in one short day, now he is bereft of
health. The nature of his bodily ailment meant terrible
fever and excruciating pain. Nothing is more wearing
than pain. Job sat down among the ashes, and in absolute
misery scraped himself with a piece of broken pottery. No
wonder!

Even his wife urged him to curse God and die, such was
his misery. But Job did not sin. He took the ground that
as he had received good from God, so should he receive
evil.

Then three friends, Eliphaz the Temanite, Bildad the
Shuhite, and Zophar the Naamathite, came to comfort
Job. So struck were they at his deplorable condition and
grief, that with Oriental patience they sat silent for seven
days and nights. At last they opened their mouths, and
with striking beauty of speech they practically told Job
that in spite of his reputation for uprightness, there must
be some hidden departure from the way of the Lord on
his part to account for his misfortunes. Job stoutly
defended himself. Backwards and forwards, charge and
counter charge were made, till at last Job's vehement self-
vindication had silenced his three friends. He ended up
with these eloquent words,

" 'If my land cries out against me, and its furrows weep together; if I have eaten its fruit without money, or caused its owners to lose their lives; then let thistles grow instead of wheat, and weeds instead of barley.' The words of Job are ended" (Job 31:38-40).

At this point a new voice is heard, that of Elihu, the Buzite, a younger man than Job and his three friends. He vehemently asks Job why does he contend with God? He accuses Job of thinking that his righteousness is more than God's. At the end of a long impassioned speech, the LORD himself speaks out of the whirlwind. He asks Job many questions as to his powers, and shows how weak and foolish he is.

At last Job sees himself in his true light in the presence of God. In a few broken sentences, ending with a complete acknowledgment of what he really was in God's holy sight, he plumbed the depth of repentance.

"I have heard of You by the hearing of the ear, but now my eye sees You. Therefore I abhor myself, and repent in dust and ashes" (Job 42:5-6).

Would Job have ever got to that length had he not gone through the terrible ordeal, we have so faintly described? Satan cruelly battered Job, only to produce in him that which was pleasing to God, even the acknowledgment of what he was in God's holy sight.

"Indeed we count them blessed who endure. You have heard of the perseverance of Job and seen the purpose of the Lord—that the Lord is very compassionate and merciful" (James 5:11).

As far as temporal things were concerned Job in the end acquired, under God's good hand, the double of what he had lost. Seven sons and three daughters came to lighten his home, an implication surely that the ones he had lost did not die like the beast of the field. In the end he had double, ten in Heaven and ten on earth. But spiritually and morally what a triumph for God, and what an untold blessing for Job, a blessing beyond words.

We began our brief history of Job under the heading, "God can use Satan for blessing". This may have been startling to some readers. We may add further support for our heading by drawing attention to the case of the incestuous man in the assembly at Corinth, whose sin was of such a nature that excommunication from the Christian assembly was necessary for the purging out of the evil in their midst. We read:

> "Deliver such a one to Satan for the destruction of the flesh, that his spirit may be saved in the day of the Lord Jesus" (1 Corinthians 5:5).

One might have imagined that to be delivered to Satan would mean the ruin, soul and body, of the unfortunate man. But here it is definitely stated, that it was for the object of "the destruction of the flesh", and for his ultimate salvation. Satan may surely overshoot the mark in his hatred against God and His people, and bring about just the opposite of what he desires, and be the instrument in God's hand of great blessing for God's people.

We also learn, God allowing it, that Satan can control fire, wind and the actions of men to carry out his wicked plans. In the case of Job, fire came down from heaven; a great wind struck the house where Job's sons and daughters were feasting; Job himself was afflicted with boils. The Sabeans and Chaldeans were instrumental in taking livestock on that terrible fateful day.

As to bringing diseases upon man, we read in the New Testament that which confirms that it is possible.

> "So ought not this woman, being a daughter of Abraham, *whom Satan has bound*—think of it—for eighteen years, be loosed from this bond on the Sabbath?" (Luke 13:16).

THE DEVIL WALKS ABOUT AS A ROARING LION

We know some militant Christians, who are all out for fighting the Devil. It is a great mistake for the believer to do any such thing. But the Christian has to resist the onslaughts of the Devil. We read:

> "Be sober, be vigilant; because your adversary the Devil walks about like a roaring lion, seeking whom he may devour. *Resist* him, steadfast in the faith, knowing that the same sufferings are experienced by your brotherhood in the world" (1 Peter 5:8-9).

The Devil seeks whom he may devour. Our part is to resist him when he attacks. There is no doubt, with the help of God, we shall get the victory, for we read,

> "*Resist* the Devil and he will flee from you" (James 4:7).

The Apostle Peter wrote about the fiery trial that came upon the early Church. The roaring lion was seen when the Christians were butchered to make a Roman holiday, and the walls of the vast Coliseum at Rome resounded with the cry, "Give the Christians to the lions"; when the dungeons of the Spanish Inquisition were filled with instruments of cruellest torture; when the fires of Smithfield raged. Today, in lands where the Gospel has some place, we may not see such extremes, but over the years hundreds of Christian pastors have languished in concentration camps and prisons, all because they stood true to the Gospel of our Lord Jesus Christ.

God give us to resist the Devil, even when he comes as a roaring lion.

SATAN AS THE SERPENT ENTICES THROUGH CRAFTINESS

Satan tried the serpent character in the Garden of Eden, and he has been using these self-same tactics ever since.

We read,

> "But I fear, lest somehow, as the serpent deceived Eve by his *craftiness*, so your minds may be corrupted from the simplicity that is in Christ" (2 Corinthians 11:3).

*   *   *   *   *

> "Put on the whole armour of God, that you may be able to stand against the *wiles* of the Devil" (Ephesians 6:11).

*   *   *   *   *

> "Lest Satan should take advantage of us; for we are not ignorant of his *devices*" (2 Corinthians 2:11).

Satan's serpent-like tactics seen in the Garden of Eden took the form of insinuating that God was not altogether good, and in putting his (Satan's) word boldly against God's, in enlarging on the advantages that would accrue to our first parents, if they would but partake of the fruit of the forbidden tree, and alas! he succeeded all too well, but not finally. But Satan's craftiness is seen at its height when he assumes the *religious* rôle. Scripture solemnly warns us as to this:

> "Satan himself transforms himself into an angel of light. Therefore it is no great thing if his ministers

also transform themselves into ministers of righteousness, whose end will be according to their works" (2 Corinthians 11:14-15).

It is to be expected that the poison offered by Satan, or his ministers, will have enough truth mixed up with it to render its presence unsuspected and undetected.

So we find much literature, filled with Bible quotations, appearing very pious and attractive, being pressed upon the Christian public. Enthusiastic followers of non-Christian cults, well primed with religious talk, offer such literature in the press, on the street, or from door to door. The deadly poison is there. We refer to such non-Christian cults as Christadelphianism, Seventh Day Adventists, Jehovah's Witnesses, Christian Science, Mormons—all unsound on the fundamentals of the Christian faith, especially on the Person of our adorable Lord, as "God manifest in the flesh", and the atoning character of His work upon the cross of Calvary.

Another way in which Satan is posing as an angel of light is in the Oxford Group (later known as Moral Re-Armament and, more recently, Initiatives of Change). At the bottom this movement is unitarian, making man his own Saviour, and limiting Christ to be an Example to be followed. Whilst He surely is this to His people, it must be preceded by and founded on belief in Christ as Saviour, whose precious blood cleanses from all sin. There can be no other foundation than this. To get a man to alter his life apart from belief in Christ as Saviour, and the work of the Holy Spirit in the heart, is simply to make it harder to win him for Christ. In plain language, the teaching of the Oxford Group only makes a man satisfied with a swept and empty house, and renders him far from proof against the awful snares of the Devil.

We come now to what is the most terrible attack on Christianity, beside which these non-Christian cults pale into insignificance. If Satan comes as an angel of light, and his ministers camouflage themselves as ministers of righteousness, we must be prepared for the presentation of the evil in very attractive and apparently pious form.

Becoming popular amongst theologians from the mid-eighteenth century, there emerged what is commonly called Higher Criticism, or Modernism. Under the plea of fuller light, of more accurate scholarship, it has succeeded in undermining the fundamentals of the Christian faith. This criticism originated in Germany, passed over to Scotland, and then spread everywhere. From many a pulpit, from many scholarly lips, the evil teaching has been doing its terrible work. The stock-in-trade of out-and-out infidels, such as Tom Paine, Charles Bradlaugh, Col. Robert G. Ingersoll, who were at least honest in not professing to be Christians, has been set forth from Christian pulpits by those who have taken the oath of loyalty to the Scriptures. What infidels did outside, they are doing inside. Infidels made frontal attacks. Modernists and Higher Critics are engaged in pulling down the Christian structure before the very eyes of the worshippers, and within the very buildings dedicated to the Gospel of Jesus Christ.

Higher Critics, or Modernists, deny the inspiration of the Scriptures, the virgin birth, weaken the atoning character of the death of our Lord upon the cross of Calvary, and even in some cases deny the bodily resurrection of our adorable Lord.

Sadly, what Modernism did for the profession of Christianity in the nineteenth and twentieth centuries, Post-Modernism, with its distrust of the existence of objective reality and absolute truth, does in the twenty-first.

The Professors of a good many theological colleges are busy poisoning the minds of their students who, finishing their course, pass on the poison in turn to their congregations. It is enough to make angels weep; Satan in his craftiness poisoning the stream of Bible teaching at its source.

The result is that such teaching does not keep the churches full, so congregations dwindle, until at last some are beginning to see that it is only the old-fashioned Gospel of the grace of God, based on the infallible, inspired Word of God, that God can bless.

Remember we are exhorted to test the spirits, and unless there is the confession of Jesus Christ come in flesh, that is, He is "God manifest in the flesh", we may know that the testimony is not of God, however piously and pretentiously it may be offered.

Why does God allow the Devil to exist?

Why does God allow the Devil to exist? Why should he have fallen? Why should God have allowed our first parents to fall, and in their fall to drag down the whole human race? These questions were forced upon me, and distressed me, when young in the Christian faith. *I had to learn to trust God where I did not understand.* I had to learn as a start of all true learning, the concept of God as supreme, all-wise, all-loving, absolutely righteous and holy in all His ways.

In cases where we cannot understand, we may well believe that if we had the full knowledge of the case as God has, and were possessed of the wisdom and power of God, and were called upon to act, we should act exactly as God has acted.

There is a very great distinction between man and the lower creation. The lower creation is not responsible. Their lives are purely animal, governed by instinct, and therefore without responsibility. Man, the highest creation of God on this earth, was created with a will, and therefore carrying with it responsibility, and capable of communing with his Creator. If God had created man unable to depart from the path of dependence and obedience, He would have created mere automatons, will-less creatures, with no power of choice. Man so created would have been merely a superior animal with no responsibility attaching to him. We shrink from the thought of such a creation as unworthy of God, and entailing terrible loss to mankind.

We have to learn to look at circumstances in the light of our knowledge of God, and not decide on the character of God in the light of circumstances, as we see them, or think we see them.

Think of Job, who drank perhaps more deeply into the cup of overwhelming sorrow in one day than any one among fallen men. Yet he could say,

> "The LORD gave, and the LORD has taken away; blessed be the name of the LORD" (Job 1:21),

> *   *   *   *   *

> "Though He slay me, yet will I trust Him" (Job 13:15).

The God who could produce such characters as Job, Abraham, Moses, David and Isaiah in Old Testament times, and Paul, Peter, James and John in New Testament times, is a God we can trust through and through.

The mystery of Satan, and the condition of the world around us, may yet be known by us when we see light in God's light in the coming day of display. Till then let us trust our God implicitly, and never question any of His ways.

The End of Satan

We read in Scripture that

> "For this purpose the Son of God was manifested, that He might destroy the works of the Devil" (1 John 3:8).

Even in the Garden of Eden, consequent on our first parent's fall, we find the LORD God saying to Satan,

> "I will put enmity between you and the woman, and between your seed and her Seed; He shall bruise your head, and you shall bruise His heel" (Genesis 3:15).

Satan must have remembered this bruising of the heel of the woman's seed when, having urged man on to commit the greatest crime of all time in the murder of the Son of God, he found that on the third day after His dead body had been placed in the tomb—the tomb sealed, and a guard set—our Lord had risen triumphant from the grave. Satan's apparent victory was the beginning of his sure defeat. That beginning began at the cross of Calvary. The power of the Devil is annulled even now. The word, *annul*, just quoted in 1 John 3:8 as "destroy", is translated in the Authorized Version as follows:

26 times as *to loose*
1 time as *be loosing*
3 times as *unloose*
1 time as *put off*
2 times as *dissolve*
5 times as *break*
1 time as *break up*
1 time as *break down*
1 time as *melt*
2 times as *destroy.*

This choice of translations will give a cumulative idea of the meaning of the word.

That there is conflict between the people of God and spiritual wickedness is clearly stated in Scripture:

"We do not wrestle against flesh and blood, but against principalities, against powers, against the rulers of the darkness of this age, against spiritual hosts of wickedness in the *heavenly* places" (Ephesians 6:12).

The conflict goes on down the ages. The poet [James Russell Lowell (1819–1891)] has sung it in eloquent language,

> *"Truth for ever on the scaffold,*
> *Wrong for ever on the throne,*
> *Yet that scaffold sways the future,*
> *And behind the dim unknown*
> *Standeth God within the shadow,*
> *Keeping watch above His own."*

This conflict is drawing to a close. In the last days we read,

"And war broke out in heaven: Michael and his angels fought against the Dragon; and the Dragon and his angels fought, but they did not prevail, nor was a place found for them in heaven any longer. So the great Dragon was cast out, that Serpent of old, called the Devil and Satan, who deceives the whole world; he was cast to the earth, and his angels were cast out with him" (Revelation 12:7-9).

We have seen from Scripture that Satan had power to present himself before the Lord. In the New Testament we get fuller light that Satan himself is the king of the bottomless pit, and that his kingdom is highly organized for evil.

It appears from the passage just quoted that the time will come when Satan's opposition to the saints of God in this present dispensation will be brought to an end. The language of this verse is surely very figurative. It sets forth very serious conflict between satanic and heavenly powers. It is connected, doubtless, with the time of the second coming of our Lord to rapture His church to glory.

Revelation 12 is parenthetic, describing in highly symbolic language, the history of the Jewish nation in relation to the birth of Christ, and what that meant. The Man Child (Christ) is brought forth, and is caught up to the throne of God, consequent as we know on the death and resurrection of our Lord. The Christian era is not taken account of in this Scripture, the subject being Christ *in relation to the Jewish nation.* But once the Christian era closes, as it does at the rapture of the church, then the history of the Jewish nation will be prominent again, and the prophecies concerning the nation in the last days will be fulfilled.

So we find the woman (the people of Israel) flies into the wilderness, into a place prepared for her of God, and there fed for 1260 days, that is 3½ years (counting the prophetic years as consisting of 360 days), the time of the great tribulation, prophesied by Daniel, and again by our Lord when He spoke of the destruction of Jerusalem.

At the end of this time under satanic influence the nations will mass themselves against the Holy Land, resulting in the great battle of Armageddon, and the raising of the siege of Jerusalem, our Lord setting up His earthly kingdom as King of the Jews, and as Son of Man over the whole earth.

Then we read of an angel coming down from Heaven, having the key of the bottomless pit in his hand,

> "He laid hold of the Dragon, that Serpent of old, who is the Devil and Satan, and bound him for a thousand years; and he cast him into the bottomless pit, and shut him up, and set a seal on him, so that he should deceive the nations no more till the thousand years were finished. But after these things he must be released for a little while" (Revelation 20:2-3).

The millennial reign of our Lord will cease at the end of 1,000 years when Satan will be loosed. Infuriated more than ever, he will deceive the nations, Gog and Magog (Russia and allies) being specifically mentioned. Vast forces come against Jerusalem when fire will come down from God, and the last great act of rebellion against God will come to a sudden and ignominious end.

> "And the Devil, who deceived them, was cast into the lake of fire and brimstone where the beast and the false prophet are. And they will be tormented day and night for ever and ever" (Revelation 20:10).

This will be the end of the Great Adversary.

May this slight sketch of Satan's origin, character, and doom be helpful to the reader. Scripture throws light on these things, and it is well for us to gain what help we can from it. Not all subjects in Scripture are pleasant, but all are profitable, and for our learning.

All we have been considering is worked out in the brief history of this world.

> "With the Lord one day is as a thousand years, and a thousand years as one day" (2 Peter 3:8).

We end with the Apostle Paul's magnificent outburst:

> "Oh, the depth of the riches both of the wisdom and knowledge of God! How unsearchable are His judgments and His ways past finding out! 'For who has known the mind of the LORD? Or who has become His counsellor?' 'Or who has first given to Him and it shall be repaid to him?' For of Him and through Him and to Him are all things, to whom be glory for ever. Amen" (Romans 11:33-36).

To which wonderful ascription of belief in every action of our God, may we all add our humble, deep-felt and worshipping AMEN.

OTHER BOOKS FROM SCRIPTURE TRUTH PUBLICATIONS

UNDERSTANDING CHRISTIANITY SERIES:

"COMFORTED OF GOD" BY A J POLLOCK (EDITOR)

ISBN 978-0-901860-63-7 (paperback)
110 pages; April 2010

THE RESURRECTION OF THE LORD JESUS CHRIST
BY A J POLLOCK, J D RICE (EDITOR)

ISBN 978-0-901860-94-1 (paperback)
88 pages; July 2015

UNDERSTANDING THE OLD TESTAMENT SERIES:

THE TABERNACLE'S TYPICAL TEACHING BY A J POLLOCK

ISBN 978-0-901860-65-1 (paperback)
236 pages; July 2009

Lightning Source UK Ltd.
Milton Keynes UK
UKHW01f1702260618
324819UK00006B/319/P